HANDBOOK OF
EARLY
ADVERTISING
ART

HANDBOOK OF EARLY ADVERTISING ART

MAINLY FROM AMERICAN SOURCES

by Clarence P. Hornung

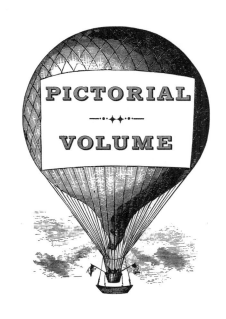

PICTORIAL
VOLUME

· THIRD EDITION ·

DOVER PUBLICATIONS, INC., NEW YORK

Published in Canada by General Publishing Company, Ltd., 30 Lesmill Road, Don Mills Toronto, Ontario.
Published in the United Kingdom by Constable and Company, Ltd.

The publisher is indebted to the following persons for their assistance in preparing this Second Edition: Massey Trotter, librarian at the New York Public Library Print Room, who searched for new material for sections on holidays and mortised cuts. Paul H. Downing, consultant on equipage, Staten Island, N. Y., who supervised the compilation of Plates 103 through 115 on horse drawn vehicles. The notes for these plates, which appear in the Appendix, were also prepared by Mr. Downing. Cyril Nast, who loaned us the drawings of his father, Thomas Nast. The New York Historical Society for permission to reproduce material from the Landauer Collection. The Staff of the New York Public Library in general and the Photographic Division in particular, for their usual admirable, indispensable assistance on many different problems. Barrows Mussey and Ruth M. Canedy, who helped locate some Christmas illustrations. The Ford Motor Company, the Packard Motor Car Company, and the Studebaker Corporation for permission to use material in the automobile section.

DOVER *Pictorial Archive* SERIES

Standard Book Number: 486-20122-8
Library of Congress Catalog Card Number: 54-9264

Manufactured in the United States of America
Dover Publications, Inc.
31 East 2nd Street
Mineola, N.Y. 11501

PREFACE TO
THIRD REVISED EDITION

The Pictorial volume of the HANDBOOK OF EARLY ADVERTISING ART has been enlarged by the addition of sixteen plates of pictures taken from Trade Advertisements of the early 19th century. They were selected to give a clear portrayal of both the exteriors and interiors of retail and manufacturing establishments of this period. They also add to the available pictures of machines, instruments, carriages, dress, etc. All of the new material was photographed directly from original prints.

1956   The Publisher

PREFACE TO
SECOND REVISED EDITION

There has been a steady demand for a new printing of the HANDBOOK OF EARLY ADVERTISING ART, and the publisher has taken this opportunity to revise and expand the work along the lines of its greatest usefulness.

The HANDBOOK's greatest usefulness has been to working artists, printers, advertising agencies, and others in the graphic arts. Expansion and revision has therefore been made mainly with the needs of these practitioners in mind. Like the old typefounders' books from which it draws so much of its material, this book has become a source of cuts, illustrations, and typography. In this respect, it is a direct lineal descendant of the type specimen books of Johnson; MacKellar, Smiths and Jordan; and other "swipe chests" of the period rather than a treatise or history of these early works.

This new edition differs from the old in the following ways:

1. Expansion of the pictorial and typographical material has been so extensive as to necessitate two separate volumes. One is devoted exclusively to illustration, and the other to typography and typographical ornamentation.

2. Almost every cut has been rephotographed from source material in order to achieve greater clarity. If certain deficiencies in clarity are still present, they reflect the well-worn quality of the original cuts.

3. Sections that have proved especially useful have been greatly expanded, and new sections have been added. Many holidays lend themselves to nostalgic presentation, and therefore, new cuts have been added to the sections on food and drink (Thanksgiving) and patriotic emblems (Independence Day). The section of Christmas cuts appears for the first time. In gathering material for the Christmas section, it was necessary to use sources other than the typefounders' catalogues because the growth of Christmas is a twentieth-century phenomenon. Christmas illustrations appear to have played a very minor role in advertising and selling in the nineteenth century. However, the publisher feels that in going to non-advertising sources, he is following in the footsteps of the nineteenth-century typefounders who readily appropriated cuts from spelling books and periodicals for similar purposes.

CONTENTS

TROY, BALLSTON
AND
SARATOGA,

DAILY LINE OF
COACHES.

This line will commence running on the first day of July, leaving each place at half past 8 A. M. every day. Passengers wishing to travel from Saratoga to Lebanon Springs, will find this line not only the most expeditious but cheapest.

Passengers for Pittsfield, Northampton and Hartford by taking this line will dine at Troy, lodge at Pittsfield, and arrive at Hartford early the next day. The road is now put in the best order, and all that is now wanting is that liberality which the establishment merits.

☞ *Seats taken at G. W. Wilcox's,* York House, *Saratoga,* and at all the Principal Houses in Troy.

L. V. & J. B. REED, Proprietors.
J. S. KEELER, *Agent,* Troy.
S. DEXTER, *Agent,* Saratoga.

TROY, JUNE 25, 1834.

N. B. On the arrival of the **ERIE** or **CHAMPLAIN**, Parties can be accommodated with coaches to Saratoga or Ballston the same evening.

Printed by Kemble & Hooper—Troy Budget Office.

EARLY NINETEENTH CENTURY POSTER

Among the first users of printed announcements, both for outdoor use and newspaper advertising, were the many coach lines connecting important cities. This poster measuring 11 by 15 inches, shows a large woodcut by J. H. Hall, with border of typographic ornaments. *Landauer Collection.*

PART 1

The beginnings of advertising during colonial days

Let us trace the flow of advertising to its Colonial sources, following the main stream, and forgetting the lesser tributaries for the moment. The first major group of advertising forms stems from outdoor examples such as signboards, tavern signs, toll and gate signs and notices displayed on buildings and in public places. There is an essential tactical distinction between this and all other forms of advertising—more than mere differences between a fixed and mobile position. The onlooker must come to the point of display in order that the advertisement may register its message. The range of effectiveness may be considered anywhere from six feet to a hundred yards, depending, of course, upon strategic position, shape and size. The descendants of this form of display are the outdoor painted bulletins, road signs, printed and lithographed posters from single sheets to twenty-four sheets, point-of-sale display material, streetcar and bus cards, painted banners and streamers, electric and spectacular advertising of all kinds. Chronologically, this category of advertising precedes all others, just as its European counterparts, the signboards of England and the Continent, were preceded by the early house signs of ancient Rome and Pompeii.

Newspapers and periodicals comprise the second group, revolving around the process of "space insertions" in regularly recurrent publications. In terms of twentieth-century advertising this is a huge classification, but in terms of Colonial backgrounds, the field is a very limited one. The forerunners of our newspapers were modest folios originally called "news-letters," issued weekly for the better part of the Eighteenth Century. Not until the close of this century was the "daily" born to the American public, and then, but for the interval of its appearance, it offered no difference from the weeklies and semi-weeklies. The magazines of the earliest post-Revolutionary years were feeble efforts that met with universal failure. Not a single publication of this type survived its formative period. Among the many reasons for this failure were a general misunderstanding of the literary tastes and needs of the people, the real purposes of a periodical, the scarcity of paper and the general illiteracy throughout the nation.

In the third group of early advertising media arrayed for the purpose of comparative study, are the many miscellaneous products of the press—the strict province of the printer and his skill and taste. This world of graphic ephemera includes all manner of shapes and forms used in the business of advertising and selling: trade cards, invoices and bills of lading, handbills and broadsides, removal announcements, descriptive leaflets, tags and labels, tickets of admission, stagecoach schedules and clipper ship sailings, anti-slavery and recruiting posters—these and all other printing needs used in business and industry go to make up this group under consideration.

In the field of Colonial newspapers, it was Benjamin Franklin, who, in connection with the publication of his newspaper, *The Pennsylvania Gazette,* in 1726, conceived the idea of adding spice and interest to his pages with the introduction of small illustrations. These were miniature one and one-half-inch stock cuts of sailing vessels engraved on wood, which were inserted into the otherwise dry announcements of cargo shipments or passenger accomodations. Later, single column cuts for special advertisers were made, undoubtedly under Franklin's personal direction. These included a representation of a pair of spectacles for an optical ad, an emblem of the "Sign of the Blue Hand" for a glove maker, and a very ornamental border frame in the manner of London tradesmen's cards for a retail merchant. These were the first semblances of store advertising as we recognize it today. From these humble beginnings there developed a whole group of small pictorial illustrations including books, horses, hats, clocks, furniture, hardware, etc. Each of these special cuts served as an index to the subject matter of the ad, thus identifying the contents in much the same way as the signboard designated the residence of a tradesman, craftsman or hostelry. Franklin had the vision to foresee how much these illustrations meant to the appearance and sale of his newspapers, as well as to the merchants concerned. His pioneering efforts may not have received the full attention they deserve; but let us not forget that Franklin was not only the patron saint of advertising in America, but may well be considered the father of advertising art.

The rise of the newspapers and early directory advertising

NEWSPAPER advertising celebrated its centennial anniversary within the first few years of the Nineteenth Century. The practice and technique of placing regular advertising had developed considerably, but physically the ad had changed little since the first insertions made their appearance in the *Boston News-Letter* of 1704. There were definite reasons why this growth was halted, why the improvements made under the guidance of John Dunlap in his paper, *The Pennsylvania Packet and General Advertiser,* were temporarily lost. Dunlap, who started publishing in Philadelphia in 1771, had greatly encouraged a consciousness on the part of advertisers and he was the first to emphasize the dictum "It pays to advertise." Consideration was given to the needs of the advertiser — an entirely new philosophy in commercial publishing — as advertisements were placed in preferred positions ahead of news of government and politics. Thumbnail cuts of houses for sale, sailing vessels and runaway slaves had been featured in larger sizes than ever before. The illustrations used served to identify the stores and merchants by recognizable emblems: a spinning wheel to mark the dry goods merchant; a mortar and pestle for the druggist; a pair of spectacles or a watch for the jeweler; an open book for the stationer or bookseller. From thumbnail cuts they soon grew to sizable proportions until some dominated the ads in full column width. The *Advertiser* started as a weekly, but within a few years had attracted such a following and steady volume of ads that finally, in 1784, it appeared as a daily, a notable gain that could largely be attributed to the extensive columns of advertising and incidental illustrated matter.

Dunlap's success in the closing quarter of the Eighteenth Century was destined to a short life. Conditions beyond his control limited publishing activities. The shortage of paper and the urgent need for conserving space in the tabloid-sized papers accounted for this setback that was to delay the full flowering of newspaper advertising illustration for almost three-quarters of a century. The roster of new advertisers and the volume of linage increased steadily, but the insertions were rigidly confined to small notices. The right-about reversal again brought back cuts to minimum sizes and the general tenor of advertising sections was levelled to a neat, but monotonous order. With the turn of the century and the decades following, the style of advertising became known as "the legal notice period in display."

The darkness that descended was not without its silver lining. The scarcity of newsprint does not seem to have extended into the general field of book publishing. Paper mills and printers were springing up in many of the towns that had never before known such industries. Juveniles, chap-books, school and spelling books began to appear in quantities, whereas previously, these had largely been imported from England.

While newspaper make-up was thus sliding back into a period of decadence, there developed a new and novel advertising medium that was destined to influence the course of commercial wood engraving and encourage the engravers striving so desperately to earn a scant livelihood. Population increases in the leading seaport cities had made such particularly rapid gains that some census publication was necessary. At the time, Philadelphia, queen city of the colonies and seat of Revolutionary government, took the lead in many matters of general, cultural and business interest. Her population had reached the high figure of about 50,000 and some listing of inhabitants and merchants was necessary. The earliest city directory appeared in Philadelphia in 1794, published by Hardie. It listed, in alphabetical order, the townspeople and their trades, and reported on the progress of the city in a dry volume of some 240 pages. After an interval of eight years, James Robinson appeared as publisher, calling his enterprise *The Philadelphia Directory, City and County Register, including Almanac.* These directories soon became annual affairs, sold on subscription only, deriving their revenue without benefit of advertising. The first use of advertising pages with accompanying illustrations, paving the way modestly for the millions of mercantile, mail-order and telephone directories that have become so integrated with our modern requirements, occurred in 1818. In that year, John A. Paxton, who had been associated with Robinson in his earlier ventures, issued a greatly improved directory including an important section called *Paxton's Philadelphia Annual Advertiser,* replete with 67 full-page ads in great variety. This volume marks a notable achievement and point of departure in advertising; for the first time between the covers of a book we find attractive, well-designed woodcuts on most of the advertisements, including illustrations of store fronts, carriages, wagons, trunks, boots and shoes, books, millinery, bells, pianos, violins and sundry vignettes decorated with patriotic motifs,

BOLIVAR HOUSE,   **WILLIAM CARELS.**

Bolivar House.

ADJOINING THE ARCADE.

No. 203,

CHESNUT STREET.

Where the subscriber keeps constantly on hand choice

WINES AND LIQUORS

Warranted pure and unadulterated, which he will furnish to families, if desired, by the Demijohn or otherwise.

He will also furnish Dinners or Suppers

For private parties or Societies, by giving timely notice.

WILLIAM CARELS.

WM. COUPLAND'S

LIVERY STABLES,

Harmony Street,

RUNNING FROM THIRD TO FOURTH,

Between Chesnut and Walnut Streets,

PHILADELPHIA.

HORSES AND CARRIAGES,.......BAROUCHES.

GIGS, SADDLE HORSES, &c.

TO HIRE.

HORSES TAKEN IN AT LIVERY.

Travellers Accommodated on the most reasonable terms.

JOHN B. KREYMBORG,

QUILL

Manufacturer

95 *South Second* street,

(Opposite the Merchants' Coffee-House, Philad.)

MANUFACTURES ALL KIND OF QUILLS,

Dutch, English, German, and Opaque,

FROM $2 50 TO 30 $ PER 1000.

SWAN AND CROW QUILLS,

at various prices.

He also offers for sale, and keeps constantly on hand, at Manufacturers prices, a large stock of

GRENVILLE'S CHEMICAL INK POWDER,

Warranted superior for immediate production of Jet Black Ink.

ALSO, SUPERIOR SEALING WAX,

Warranted to burn free and stick well, of various colours, viz. Light and Dark Blue, Light and Dark Green, Yellow, Brown, Gold, Rose, Flesh, Orange, &c.

MAMMOTH.

Philadelphia Museum,

IN THE UPPER PART OF THE

ARCADE,

CHESNUT STREET, (ABOVE SIXTH.)

OPEN throughout the day, and ILLUMINATED every evening.

Admittance 25 Cents.

This Museum is the oldest and largest establishment in the United States, and contains immense collections of the Animal and Mineral kingdoms of nature, from all parts of the world. These are all beautifully arranged, so as to enable the visitor to study the objects with the greatest advantage. The collection of implements and ornaments of our aboriginal tribes is very extensive and interesting, and the Cabinet of Antiquities, and Artificial Curiosities, is not less worthy of attention. In addition to the ordinary attractions of a Museum, there is in this a very large collection of the Portraits of American Statesmen and Warriors of the Revolution, and of the most distinguished scientific men of Europe and America.

The Founder, C. W. Peale, desirous of securing the Museum permanently in this city, obtained an act of Incorporation, by which the stability of the Institution is insured. The act of Incorporation secures the use of the Museum in perpetuity to the city, and authorizes the Stockholders to appoint annually five trustees, who meet quarterly to regulate the business of the Institution. Nothing can be removed from the Institution under a penalty, and forfeiture of double the value of the thing removed; hence donations may be made with certainty on the part of the donors, that the articles placed in the Museum will always remain for the public good.

BOOK PAGE ADVERTISEMENTS IN 1829

Typical are these reduced page announcements from Desilvers' "Philadelphia Directory and Stranger's Guide." The cuts are by local wood engravers made expressively for these ads.

especially the American eagle.

In the following year's directory there is included a handsomely designed ad in cartouche style for George Gilbert, engraver, of 13 South Fourth Street, Philadelphia. Throughout the volume his mark "G" appears on many cuts, testifying to his handiwork and proving that these cuts were ordered for the publication.

Paxton, unlike the later directory publishers who utilized stock foundry cuts, may be considered a pioneer in the book publishing and advertising field, and may well have supplied the impetus upon which the progressive Philadelphia foundries established an assortment of cuts to be sold for users of printing throughout the country.

In New York, Longworth's *American Almanac and New York Register and City Directory* started publication in 1801. For the first ten years of its existence, few ads appeared and these, for the most part, remained unillustrated. By comparison with the Philadelphia directories, Longworth's annuals were very backward from an advertising viewpoint. In Boston, John West published the first directory in 1803. Stimpson's *Directory Advertiser* appeared years later—and became a regular annual publication with ads in the customary "card" and announcement style. The 1833 edition, however, contained a copperplate engraving insert by Nathaniel Dearborn, preceding the usual advertising section, a custom that had first been introduced by Paxton in his 1818 Philadelphia Directory.

In the 1834 edition of Stimpson's there appeared one of the earliest advertisements of a corporate group of graphic artists, ready and anxious to solicit business under the strange trade name of the "Boston Bewick Company." This announcement read:

"Ready to receive orders on behalf of the company for engraving in wood, steel and copperplate and for letterpress and copperplate in all its branches. The corporation, having purchased stock and tools of the American Engraving and Printing Company, are prepared to execute orders in the best possible man-

ner, with promptness and on reasonable terms. The Boston Bewick Company, having been established by the artists, and being incorporated by an Act of the Legislature, it is believed they will not only do credit to the name of the "restorer of the Art of Engraving on Wood" (the late Thomas Bewick) but be able to do business to great advantage to their customers and to the public generally. . . . Orders for Wood Cuts, Designs and Drawing, Maps and Charts, Cards of every description, Diplomas and Seals, Copperplate and Xylographic Printing, Book and Job Printing. Address to: Freeman Hunt, Agent of B. B. Co., 47 Court Street, Boston. Signed by Abel Bowen, Alonzo Hartwell, John H. Hall, William Croome, George W. Boynton, John C. Crossman, Daniel H. Craig. Dated Boston, Mass., June 21, 1834."

Wood engraving—the principal medium for early advertising art

IT IS by no mere accident that we find the art of wood engraving the principal vehicle by which early advertising illustration was conveyed in print. In Europe, four hundred years before, the earliest woodcuts first served a public hungry for pictures in any form. These were used in litur-

ILY   CH

dity on the patent Napier Press---but its extensive circulation requires that Advertise

☞ ALL ADVERTISEMENTS PAID FOR BY THE SQUARE, ARE INSERTED ALSO IN THE SATURDAY COURIER.

PHILADELPHIA, WEDNESDAY, APRIL 27, 1831.

To Let for a Short Time.

A neat two story brick house. No. 168 South Third, near Pine street, for 8 or 10 weeks. Rent low. Inquire at No. 14 South Fourth street, or on the premises.
WILLIAMS & HOLLAWAY.
april 25--dtf

ADAMS' PATENT SWELLED
Beam Windlass Bedsteads.

THE above Bedsteads are put together without screws, and by means of the Windlass and Swelled Beam, the Sacking is kept crowding and elastic at all times with the least possible trouble, which is impossible to obtain on those made any other way.

Pure curled Hair Matrasses constantly on hand.

BOSTON SPRING-SEAT ROCKING CHAIRS, Venitian, Transparent and India Blinds. Also, a great variety of ornaments and materials for interior decoration, constantly on hand, and Upholstery Work of every description executed with neatness, punctuality and despatch, by

J. HANCOCK & Co.
S. W. corner of Third and Walnut streets.

P. S. J H. & Co grateful for past favours, they hope, by constant attention to business, and a desire to please, by keeping the richest articles in their line, to obtain future patronage.   april 21--1y

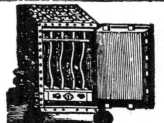

Superior Patent Fire Proof Composition
CHESTS.

THE subscriber by constant study and unremitted industry in this art, has made for this last twelve months a rapid discovery in fire-proof materials. He continues to manufacture the above article at as low prices as they can be purchased in any part of the United States.
JOHN SCOTT.
No. 1 Lodge street, north of Pennsylvania Bank. All orders thankfully received and sent to any part of the United States.   april 25--tf

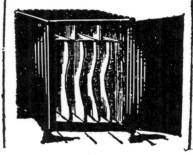

COTTON.

75 BALES Cotton just landed from brig Yellow Bird, from New Orleans. For sale by
DAVID B. RISING,
april 25--d1w   No. 35 South Front street.

INCORRUPTIBLE
Porcelain Teeth.

THE Subscriber respectfully informs the public, that he sets Porcelain, or any other Teeth the person may desire, on moderate terms. The approved Porcelain Teeth, which he manufactures of any shade to correspond with the natural ones, will retain their original colour for any length of time, and are not decomposed by acids. Those set by him will be warranted to stand, and be as serviceable as any thing of the kind can be made.

Operations on the Teeth performed on reasonable terms.

SAMUEL CHAMBERLAIN, Dentist,
No. 47 North Eighth, 4th door below Arch street.
april 20--tf

Thomas Gibson, Plumber,

RESPECTFULLY informs his friends and the public in general, that he carries on the House and Ship Plumbing, in all its branches, at No. 136 North Third street, where he has constantly on hand Hydrants, of various descriptions, Patent Hatter's Plank Kettles to burn Lehigh Coal of the newest construction, Water Closets, Baths, Tubs, Shower Baths, Lead and Iron Pipes, Retorts for Bleaching and all other Cynical apparatus, furnished at the shortest notice, and also, Sheet Lead of various sizes on the most reasonable terms.   THOMAS GIBSON,
jan 5--ly   136 North Third street.

Venitian Blind Warehouse,

N. E. CORNER OF CHESNUT AND SECOND STREETS.

THE subscriber respectfully informs the citizens of Philadelphia and vicinity, that he has constantly on hand a very extensive assortment of Venitian Window Blinds, of various patterns, sizes, and colours, now extant all of which will be sold wholesale or retail for cash or city acceptances, 25 per cent. lower than any other house in this city.
SAM. K. BARTLESON, Agt.
april 4--tf

470 Silver Watches,

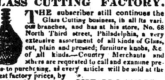

FROM $3.50 to $10 each, warranted to run. Patent Levers, Gold and Silver of the most approved makers, 1500 pair Gold Ear Rings, from 75 cts. to $30.00 per pair, 2,100 Breast Pins and Finger Rings from 50 00 to $30 per doz. A variety of fancy goods Steel and Gilt, Silver Spoons, Spectacles and Thimbles, &c. &c. For wholesale at reduced prices and on liberal terms. Most of the above goods manufactured and for sale by B. ROBINSON, at his store, No. 62 Market street, between Second and Third streets, one door above Strawberry street, south side.
feb 23--3m

GLASS CUTTING FACTORY.

THE subscriber still continues the Glass Cutting business, in all its various branches, and has at his store, No. 68 North Third street, Philadelphia, a very extensive assortment of all kinds of Glass, cut, plain and pressed; furniture knobs, &c of all kinds.--Country Merchants and others are requested to call and examine previous to purchasing, as every article will be sold at the lowest factory prices, by
oct 21--tf   RICHARD S. RISLEY.

G. MEYER,
Cabinet, Grand and Square
PIANO FORTE
MANUFACTURER,
NO. 50 SOUTH FIFTH STREET,
Two doors North of Prune street.

A CARD.

THE public at large is respectfully informed that a very large assortment of Caps and Stocks, of every description, may now be obtained at the most reasonable prices, by applying to
N. SYLVESTER,
8 South Sixth street.

Hair Cloth in every variety, French and American manufacture, made into Caps or Stocks at 3 hours notice. A large quantity of these articles constantly ready made.

N. B. The subscriber's store is No. 8 South Sixth street, 4 doors below Market, and opposite the side of the Schuylkill Bank   april 25--tf

OLD ESTABLISHMENT,
OPPOSITE GIRARD'S BANK.

A GOOD assortment of HATS, at No. 61 South 3d street, which will be sold at fair prices.

☞ Those who wish a hat of any quality or fashion whatever, finished, can be accommodated, and should the article not please when finished, there will be no obligation on the part of those who order to take it.   april 8--tf

HATS,
WHOLESALE AND RETAIL,
No. 41 South Third Street,
NEAR CONGRESS HALL.

JOHN C. DYER offers for sale, HATS of every description, of superior qualities, and cheap. J. C. D. particularly invites the attention of the public to his four dollar Hats, which, for beauty, durability and cheapness, are not surpassed by any in the city.

JOHN C. DYER respectfully informs his friends and the public, that he has opened a store in his line of business, at the above named place, where he intends to keep constantly on hand a general assortment of HATS, which he will sell as low as they can be purchased in the city.   march 5--6mo

CITY HAT WAREHOUSE.
Superior Hats, at $4 25.
Notice to the Fashionable and Economical.

THE closing of the winter calls to our recollection the enjoyment of spring. Its delightful promenades, &c. &c. Fully aware of the importance of Meeting Nature, by clothing ourselves with every thing beautiful, the proprietor of the City Hat Warehouse offers Hats at the moderate price of FOUR DOLLARS and twenty-five cents, which he will warrant to retain their color, shape and superior gloss, and which, for beauty, durability, lightness and elasticity and economy, are not exceeded, if equalled by any heretofore sold at 8 or 9 dollars. As there has been a number of the trade who have been continually trying to injure this Economical and Fashionable Establishment, the proprietor would invite the public to call and examine, before they purchase. He has received the latest Fashions, and beautiful style of the late curl worn by the most fashionable of London and Paris, and has been greatly admired by all who have seen its peculiar neatness. As there was a number of gentlemen disappointed in not receiving their hats, they are respectfully invited to call and receive them; as the subscriber has made arrangements so that none can be disappointed. All at tea suited. No deviation in price, as small profits will not allow of it.   P. BREMOND,
61 Chesnut street, formerly Fletcher & Co.
april 23--tf74

FOR NEW YORK.

EVERY accommodation is afforded to passengers with the Mail, which is carried to NEW YORK in REESIDE'S splendid RED COACHES; spirited horses, and careful drivers. The GUARD accompanies the Mail. Apply at the Red Office, No. 24 South Third street.   jn 4--tf

NIGHT BOAT
For BALTIMORE.

THIS line will commence for the season, on Wednesday, April the 13th, at half past 12 o'clock, from Chesnut street wharf. Passengers conveyed through the Chesapeake and Delaware Canal, and arrive in Baltimore by the Steamboat Carroll of Carrollton. Fare, $4. Baggage at the risk of the owner thereof.
april 13--tf

NEWSPAPER DISPLAY WITH PICTORIAL INSERTS

In this page from the Philadelphia Chronicle of 1831, we see a variety of stock woodcuts from current offerings of the type foundries. Philadelphia papers pioneered with the use of cuts since Franklin's day.

gical and secular works, especially in chronicles, books of hours, bibelots and, at a somewhat later date, as illustrations for the classics. Because they could be bold and vigorous in style or delicate and sensitive in line, the scope of these woodcuts was made to include all types of printing in which a pictorial effect was required. The printer soon learned to depend upon the woodcutter to supply the forceful effects that either his typography, bookmaking or editorship failed to achieve. Furthermore, since the block was fashioned to type height and thus could be locked into position along with movable types, it became an adjunct of great economy and usefulness. Experience indicated that these cuts stood up well and showed but slight wear after sizable editions had been run off.

In this country the first wood engravers who served commerce could enjoy no illusions about practicing a fine art—the need was a purely functional one. The engraver received an occasional assignment from the printer or publisher, rarely another source. There was little glory to the task, much less recompense. Pioneer that he was, the artist labored under more than the usual difficulties: poor tools, poor materials, lack of proper training, insufficient patronage and a pittance for his efforts. Little wonder that the first results to be seen in our early newspapers showed up so crudely.

Towards the close of the Eighteenth Century in England, a renascence in the art of wood engraving had set in that was soon to be transported to and take root on American soil. Under the leadership of Thomas Bewick, engraver-naturalist of Newcastle-on-Tyne, a new school of "white line" engraving flourished, spreading its influence throughout the length and breadth of the British Kingdom. Bewick, as a lad of seventeen, first started illustrating books in the year 1770, and it was not long before his talents were recognized and rewarded. Publishers sought him out for the clear brilliance of his designs and the exquisite graphic qualities of his vignettes that seemed to grow out of text and typography. By the end of the century his hand had already embellished some 130 volumes, the most renowned of which were his *Fables, History of British Birds* and *Quadrupeds*. It was only natural that copies of Bewick's works should find their way across to the colonies and thus, into the hands of a young doctor named Alexander Anderson, who, while studying medicine, was busy experimenting with engraving on metal.

Anderson was born in New York on the twenty-first of April, 1775. While still at school, he amused himself by copying engravings on crudely rolled sheets of copper pennies made to his order by a local silversmith. The young student was eager to follow a career of engraving, but his father dissuaded him from such a course. At fourteen, he was apprenticed to Dr. Joseph Young, and for five years continued to study anatomy and medicine. During this period young Anderson occupied his leisure hours with engraving of a miscellaneous character—working on anything from dog collars to book frontispieces. W. J. Linton, in his excellent *History of Wood-Engraving in America*, describes Anderson's start as follows:

"He made trials of boxwood and this changed his course. . . . The first mention of its use for gain occurs in his diary under the date of June 25, 1793, when he engraved a tobacco stamp. *A few days afterward,* he agreed to engrave *on wood* one hundred geometrical figures for S. Campbell, a New York bookseller, for fifty cents each, Campbell finding the wood. This was procured from Ruthven, a maker of carpenters' tools, who at first charged three cents apiece for the blocks, but finally asked four cents. To face the wood properly was a new, and no doubt a difficult, kind of work for him. It was *more than a year later* before Anderson ventured to engrave elaborate pictures on the wood."

A typical extract from Anderson's diary of this period informs us: "*Sept. 26.*—This morning rose at five o'clock. Took a little walk. Engraved. Employed during the chief part of the forenoon making out medicine. Came home after dinner and finished the wooden cut. Was pretty well satisfied with the impression, and so was Durell. Desired the turner to prepare the other twenty-four." And a later entry from his diary of 1798: "*April 2.*—Some days ago I proposed to A. Tiebout the publication of Bewick's *History of Quadrupeds* on the following terms. The cuts, which form a material part of the work, were to be engraved on wood by myself at the rate of half a dollar each. All other expenses were to be answered by him and each of us was to receive a proportional share of the profits. This evening he agreed to make trial of a half-sheet to be sent round with the proposals. I began to prepare the cuts."

From the foregoing statement, it will be seen that Anderson, while a pioneer of the art in this country, leaned heavily upon his British master. In fact, he re-engraved hundreds of Bewick's works for American publishers, a common custom in those pre-copyright days. Anderson forsook the practice of medicine at an early age, after the yellow fever epidemic robbed him of his entire family in 1795. He executed all manner of commissions for publishers, printers and merchants "from sheet ballads, primers, business cards, tobacconists' devices, wrappers of playing cards, diplomas and newspaper cuts of every sort, to magazines, scientific treatises and large Bibles" (according to Lossing, his biographer).

From humble beginnings at a time when he stood alone in his field, Anderson continued to produce great numbers of engravings, devoting much of his output to illustrations for book publishers. But his commercial and advertising work was by no means inconsequential. There was hardly a type of business or phase of industry for which his talents were not in demand, establishing for himself, by virtue of both variety and volume, the full-fledged right to be called not only "the father of wood engraving in America," but also the country's "first commercial artist." Considering the vast amount of work executed during his full lifetime of 95 years, of which certainly 70 were productive ones (the New York Public Library has in its collection over 8,000 proofs in old scrapbooks), the collector finds great difficulty in running down available Anderson items except in small book form. Much of his

work appeared in tiny, paper covered leaflets, principally the juveniles, spelling books and Sunday school merit awards issued in millions by the American Tract Society. His purely commercial specimens are among the rarest of antiquarian ephemera. They did abound as trade cards, billheads, seals, newspaper mastheads, label cuts, stickers and advertising trade-marks, but precious few are to be found even in the historical collections in museums and libraries.

Anderson's importance lies chiefly in his pioneering efforts and the extent of his useful purposes during the inceptive period of his craft—not in his originality or artistry.

Besides the rich heritage of work, Anderson was able to inspire a group of four pupils: Garret Lansing, William Morgan, John H. Hall, and his own daughter, Anna, who became the wife of Andrew Maverick, a copperplate engraver. Lansing received instructions in 1804, and thus became the second wood engraver in the country. He returned to Albany after a sojourn in New York, and continued to work for Anderson who sent him blocks "by the Albany sloop." Hall, who started in 1826, became active in Albany, and his name appears on some early type foundry cuts of that time. We find him re-establishing himself in New York and doing some very creditable illustrations for the *Manual of the Ornithology of the United States and Canada.* But during the California gold rush of '49, he traveled west and died soon thereafter. Morgan, another of Dr. Anderson's pupils and his favorite draughtsman, "engraved well," but he soon abandoned the graver for the pencil. Of the master's disciples, though their talents varied greatly, none was able to rise above the level of mediocrity. The seeds of the wood engraving art had now been scattered about freely, and were falling into fertile furrows, soon to give rise to a new crop of craftsmen destined to take their place in the annals of our early advertising art.

We soon find other contemporaries of

Anderson and his school in the larger cities. In Boston, there were Abel Bowen and his apprentice, Nathaniel Dearborn; in Philadelphia, William Mason and his pupil, Gilbert; in New Haven, John W. Barber. Of this group who followed Anderson, Bowen is perhaps the most important, not so much because he was the first to set up an engraving business in Boston (1812), but because he is credited with having initiated the idea of syndicating stock woodcuts through the medium of stereotyping by the type foundries. Dearborn started in business two years after Bowen, this evidently having been a sufficient period of apprenticeship for him. William Croome, another of Bowen's pupils, worked along similar lines, but he subsequently turned to designing and illustrating banknotes. Mason, who was a native of Connecticut, established himself in Philadelphia in 1810. George Gilbert, after terminating his association with his teacher, enjoyed an engraving practice of some note, being connected for a while with the American Sunday-School Union, and also doing a considerable number of fine advertising cuts such as those in Paxton's Directory for 1818 and 1819. Studying the work and the careers of these early engravers, it may safely be said that they were largely patronized by the book and tract publishing circles; both were rapidly expanding enterprises that made demands upon the few available cutters. Incidental commissions were forthcoming from printers and a few individuals who constituted what might be termed, in a very restricted sense, "a commercial market." To this must now be added an important new source of patronage, amounting at first to a mere trickle of business but later assuming proportions of steady growth.

The advent of the type foundries, along with the development of the art of stereotyping, supplied the much needed lifeblood to the printing and publishing industry. This growth from humble and modest beginnings gave root to a genuinely native graphic art—

later to blossom forth into a full flowered advertising art. The process by which this was effected—the characters who play the all-important roles—should be clearly understood at the outset, because it is through their joint and cooperative efforts that the foundations of advertising were built. First, there is the wood engraver whose designs and illustrations provide the wherewithal to embellish printed advertising matter; second, there is the stereotyper who processes the engravings and casts them in type metal so that they may be reproduced in quantities; third, there is the type founder (often, himself, the stereotyper) who catalogs, lists, sells and distributes these stock cuts to printers over a wide territory; and finally, there is the printer, purchasing these cuts from the foundries and thus making them available for use by his clients, the publishers and advertisers. This cycle, once established, became the pattern for a substantial part of the advertising art running throughout the major portion of the Nineteenth Century.

The first regular American type foundries were a product of the exciting, expansive period of the early 1800's. Their business was supplying printers, newspapers and periodicals with the mobile equipment necessary for job composition and printing of all descriptions. Type faces, quite naturally, were the mainstay of their existence, but along with these were sold many accessory items such as ornaments, printer's flowers, pictorial cuts, illustrations, astronomical, mathematical and chemical symbols, etc. In addition, the foundry sold the multitudinous odds and ends needed to equip and operate the printshop, such as hand presses, rollers, chases, stones, type cases, furniture, inks, etc. Before the establishment of the native foundries, printers were dependent upon importations from abroad, principally from Great Britain. The early use of foreign cuts, as a result, forestalled any chance of the development of a native style—in fact, many of the printed

Wilmington and New-Castle Mail.

THE SUBSCRIBERS respectfully inform the Public, and the Citizens of Wilmington and New-Castle in particular, that they have established a Stage for the purpose of carrying the Mail between the aforesaid places, and also for the conveyance of passengers and baggage....It will leave New-Castle for Wilmington, every morning between 6 and 7 o'clock, and arrive at D. BRINTON's Tavern, in time for passengers to take the 8 o'clock Stage for Philadelphia.

THE Stage will occasionally return to New-Castle in the forenoon, when a sufficient number of passengers offer, and back to Wilmington, and leave there every day for New-Castle after the arrival of the Philadelphia Stages.

Passengers may rest assured, that this establishment will be much safer and more expeditious than any heretofore established between those two Towns; having the best horses, and a careful driver.

Wilmington,
Delaware.

JOSEPH BRINGHURST, P. M. *Wilmington.*
DAVID MORRISON, P. M. *New-Castle.*

POWELL & THORP'S
WESTERN & NORTHERN

Stage & Canal Packet Boat Office,

No. 365 North Market-st. near the Mansion-Houses.

STAGES leave this office every morning and afternoon for Schenectady, Little Falls, Sacket's Harbor, Auburn, Geneva, Canandaigua, Rochester, Lewiston, Buffalo and Niagara—through in three days to Buffalo.

For CHERRY-VALLEY, COOPERSTOWN. Madison, Manlius. Syracuse and Elbridge to Auburn, every Monday, Wednesday and Friday mornings.

For WHITEHALL, (in connection with the Champlain Steam-Boats,) every Monday, Wednesday and Friday mornings, by Coaches to Fort Edward, thence to Whitehall by CANAL PACKET BOATS. *Through in One Day.*—The Steam Boat leaves Whitehall every Tuesday and Saturday, at 2 P. M. for St. Johns, where Coaches are in waiting for Montreal.

For BALLSTON and SARATOGA SPRINGS, every day, by way of Troy & Waterford, and also by way of Schenectady, thence to meet the Packet Boat at Fort Edward.—Stages also run from this Office every morning and afternoon to meet the PACKET BOATS at Schenectady. ☞ Four and two horse Extras always in readiness. POWELL & THORP, ⎰ Proprietors.
Albany, June 20, 1824. SWAN, THORP & Co. ⎱

Good Intent Line
OF COACHES.

Tri - Weekly   Line Between

KALAMAZOO, BATTLE CREEK & GRAND RAPIDS,

The PROPRIETOR has recently Stocked this Route with GOOD Horses, new Coaches and careful and experienced drivers. No pains will be spared to make this a COMFORTABLE and AGREEABLE route to travelers.
This is the nearest and BEST route, and over the best roads to

Hastings, Flat River, Saranac, and Ionia.

LEAVES Battle Creek and Kalamazoo, Tuesday, Thursday and Saturday mornings, on the arrival of the M. C. R. R. Cars from the East and West. From Battle Creek, this line passes through Ross Centre, Yorkville, Gull Prairie, and there connects with the Stages from Kalamazoo for Prairieville, Orangeville, Yankee Springs and Middleville, connecting there with Stages for Grand Rapids, which pass through Caledonia, Whitneyville and Cascade.

LEAVES GRAND RAPIDS

for Middleville, there connecting with Battle Creek and Kalamazoo Line, passing through the above named places, on Monday, Wednesday and Friday mornings, arriving at Battle Creek and Kalamazoo in time to take the Cars for the East or West, and also in time for Humphrey & Co's line of stages for the Southern Railroad.

Stages Leave & Take Passengers at all Public Houses!

Conveyances may be had at all of the principle places on the Route, to any part of the country.

Yankee Springs, Nov. 1854. C. W. LEWIS, Proprietor.

STAGECOACH ADVERTISING TAKES THE LEAD

Beginning in the early 1800's and continuing for over fifty years coach posters, cards and newspaper insertions featured stock woodcuts. These show constantly changing styles in conveyances although printers often used outdated cuts for lack of more modern ones. *Landauer Collection.*

notices in Franklin's and Dunlap's papers are essentially British in flavor. In his *Autobiography* Benjamin Franklin records the purchase by his brother, James, of both type and presses from England. Later, as manager of Keimer's press in Philadelphia, he writes: "Our printing house often wanted sorts, and there was no letter founder in America; I had seen types cast at James's in London, but without much attention to the manner; however, I now contrived a mould, made use of the letters we had as puncheons, struck the matrices in lead, and thus supply'd in a pretty tolerable way all deficiencies." Actually, the earliest pre-Revolutionary foundry was that of Christopher Sauer, or Sower, which started operations at Germantown, Pennsylvania. (Updike gives the date as 1772 in his *Printing Types,* while Thomas MacKellar, himself a founder of note, mentions the year 1735.) A few abortive and short-lived attempts at typefoundry establishments appear in 1768, 1775 and 1787. In 1796, a similar venture was started in Philadelphia by two natives of the city of Edinburgh, Archibald Binny and James Ronaldson, who later purchased the appliances for typefounding brought over by Franklin. When they issued their first specimen in 1809, it represented a milestone in the history of the craft in America. This little book, measuring 5 by 8½ inches and containing 101 cuts, was called *A Specimen of Metal Ornaments cast at the Letter Foundry of Binny & Ronaldson.* Philadelphia. Printed by Fry and Kammerer, 1809. This showing gives no type faces, but displays ornamental designs, borders, cartouches, vignettes of ships, eagles and a miscellany of unrelated cuts both large and small. The prices of cuts listed for sale range from twenty-five cents to five dollars, the latter for a heraldic composition resembling the Pennsylvania state seal. For the most part, the designs shown give evidence of foreign origin, being inspired largely from French sources similar to those exhibited in Pierre's collection of 1785. About two dozen of these cuts are undoubtedly from the hand of Dr. Anderson, the only American engraver known to have cut metal ornaments prior to the date of issue, 1809. This conclusion is further supported by the tiny initial "A" appearing on five of the bird subjects, part of a large series he engraved as book illustrations. The two large double-page folded cuts, each showing a horse led by his rider, are especially crude in design and workmanship, yet I am of the opinion they are Anderson's, as later refinements of the identical subjects appear with his name inscribed. This type of cut (Plate 96, Fig. 1) proved very popular and useful for posters announcing horse races, auctions, etc. They are continually featured in large format in subsequent foundry offerings.

In order to reach a better understanding of the beginnings of advertising art, it is necessary to turn back to the first quarter of the Nineteenth Century, to examine the functions of the early type foundries and their relation to printing. Already, there were signs of the growth of a distinct new class of printers known as job printers. They answered the needs required for commercial or social affairs; they printed trade cards, billheads, bills of lading, sailing notices, horse-racing announcements, broadsides of sales and auctions, stagecoach schedules and tickets, labels and public notices. The equipment of the printshops was crude indeed, the assortment of faces very limited. "Display faces" were unknown at the time, and such illustrative cuts as were on hand could have been acquired in only two ways: either directly from the few wood engravers who practiced in the larger cities, or through the medium of the several foundries. The latter served to interpret the needs of the printer and the wants of his customers, and furnished such cuts and types for which the demand was greatest. For the job printer's needs the foundries provided an infinite variety of letter designs, borders and miscellaneous pictorial cuts from the tiny sort to gigantic illustrations suitable for poster use. A glance at the type founders' specimen books of the 1820's and 1830's already reveals the "bestsellers" among hundreds of cuts for general sale. Leading the list of these offerings were cuts of the state seals (Plates 178-184), lottery figures and embellishments (Plate 71), patriotic motifs with the eagle in great profusion (Plates 57-66, 148), stagecoaches in varying sizes (Plates 103-115), canal boats and sailing vessels (Plates 155-166), runaway slaves and auction cuts (Plate 203), horses (Plates 90-102), domestic animals (Plates 10-22) and a broad variety of natural history subjects. A staple line of seasonal cuts and harvest scenes (Plates 4, 5) was included for almanac use. At first there was little semblance of order in the foundry specimen showings, but gradually the helter-skelter presentation gave way to classification and sequence. The tiniest cuts designed especially for restricted space and newspaper usage were shown together under the general heading of "newspaper cuts." Legal cuts such as "L. S.," indenture heads, logotypes and special designs such as "Shipped to," "Bought of," etc. formed a separate grouping. As the specimen books grew in size, they combined under one cover the three main divisions of typecast material, generally in the following order: first, a showing of text types followed by display faces; second, ornaments and borders; third, pictorial and decorative cuts. This arrangement became standard practice, but not without some exceptions.

As the printer bought more and more of these stock cuts from the various foundries, since he rarely found one source of supply adequate for all his needs, he built up a storehouse of hundreds, or even thousands, of cuts of all kinds. The problem of storage and arrangement was not inconsiderable; the accumulation of dirt and grime after years of disuse was another factor tending to give sloppy printing results. The cuts in popular demand were subjected to continual use, and as they wore down, and became nicked or damaged

from careless handling, the defects showed up noticeably. Certain cuts, however, seem to have been destined to perennial use. As we trace their individual histories and study their charmed lives, we are amazed to observe how frequently they reappear on the scene over long periods of time. To take a few isolated cases at random: a typical instance is that of a charming set of twelve vignettes depicting rural scenes throughout the seasons (Plate 5). These cuts first show up in *Knickerbocker's Almanac* in the year 1828, published by Caleb Bartlett, in New York. Their appearance in *Johnson's Type Foundry Specimen*, dated 1834, Philadelphia, gives rise to the question of whether the publisher or founder was first to issue them. Again, as text illustrations for *Introduction to Popular Lessons*, an elementary schoolbook, they appear in 1848, published by Roe Lockwood & Son, New York. At the close of the Civil War, we discover the identical series as reprints from the *Farmer's Almanac* appearing in *Eighty Years' Progress of the United States*, published in Hartford in 1867. Some sixty years thereafter, in 1926, they continue to serve as main illustrations in the *Farmer's Almanac*, thereby completing over a century of continual service. The extent and scope of their use is testimony to the remarkable vigor of the original designs, which were, in all probability, the work of Anderson. It would be difficult to find a more serviceable set of decorative compositions in any age.

Equally remarkable is the record of continual usage of some patriotic motifs, particularly certain eagle designs cast in type metal by the various foundries. Outstanding among these is one of a spread eagle (Plate 65, Fig. 6), wings aloft, the right talon clutching an American shield and olive branch, while the left grasps a set of five arrows. Its original appearance on a page headed "Eight lines pica ornaments" occurs in the catalog called *A Specimen of Printing Types cast in the Franklin Letter-Foundry of A. W. Kinsley*

& *Co., Albany, N. Y.,* issued in 1828. From then on, this ornament reaches unparalleled popularity, appearing in many competitive specimens issued during the Nineteenth Century. Johnson included it in 1834, Connor in 1851, etc. Evidently, there was little protection afforded by federal statute as this, and similar cuts, were openly appropriated and electrotyped regardless of original ownership. In more recent times, with the renewed interest stimulated by nineteenth-century type revivals, this same eagle design and many of its contemporary kin have appeared with greater frequency. The author, in an article written for the *American Artist* in 1941 entitled "The American Eagle," uses the aforementioned bird to illustrate the point of vitality in these early engraved pieces. The designers and engravers of that day achieved such brilliance in their compositions and such finesse with their graven lines that a prolonged life span of over a century was but their natural destiny.

Trade cards and announcements — precursors in the field of printing design

Wⁿ have already noted, in earlier discussions, two distinct types of early American advertising: the outdoor sign and related forms, and periodical advertising, comprising both newspapers and magazines. There remains yet a third group for consideration, that vast, uncharted realm of applied graphic art forms including trade cards, labels and other illustrated commercial printing.

Trade cards take their place prominently in the domain of ephemeral printing. The earliest known examples date from the first quarter of the Eighteenth Century. (Bella Landauer exhibits a plain, typographic card by Richard Worley, bookseller and stationer, circa 1730, in her volume, *Early American Tradecards.*) The term "card," derived from a pasteboard card, assumes importance in antiquarian parlance, designating a printed notice of goods or services for sale; it usually contains the name and address of the merchant, with some descriptive matter. There is no limitation on size or quality of paper—printed examples quite naturally required different stock from those engraved on copperplate. The pattern of trade card design follows no set formula except a conformity dictated by the medium of printing. Purely typographic ones, like that of Richard Worley cited above, were limited in early years to the paucity of material in the printer's case. If there were not enough ornaments to fill the enclosing border, the printer was obliged to improvise, throwing in all kinds of extraneous flowers including question marks, ampersands, etc. Later on, with the aid of the wood engraver, he could insert a cut of the merchant's building or shop front, or some especially engraved illustration of merchandise. The card of the New York Patent Comb Manufactury, circa 1818, includes a quaint woodcut of an elephant by Anderson, and two smaller cuts showing a tortoise and some steers, the entire scheme a bit of drollery in type arrangement by the printers, J. & J. Harper. From this point, with the development of stock offerings by the foundries, great opportunities in design were opened to the printer, who responded with an

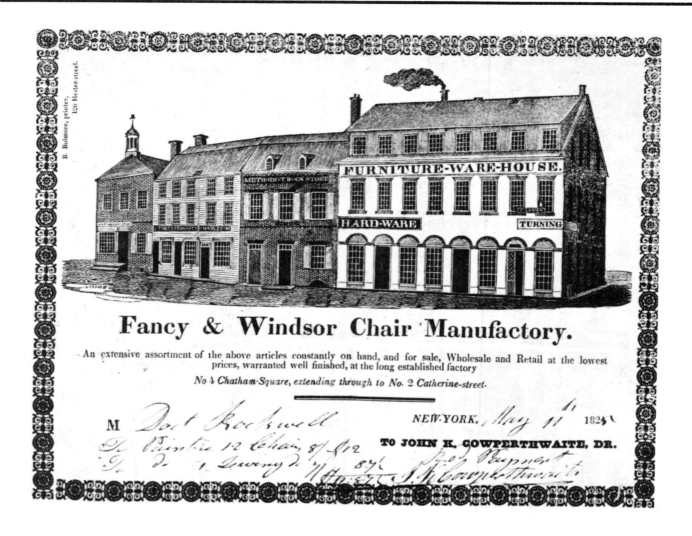

TRADECARDS OF EARLY FURNITURE MANUFACTURERS

The Cowperthwaite card of 1825 features a skilfully designed wood engraving, by Lansing, of the maker's warehouse and adjacent buildings. Surrounding type border shows a popular motif (Compare with Saratoga poster on Page viii). The Woodwell card is of Civil War period. *Landauer Collection.*

ever-widening range of variations.

It is well at this point, before examining numerous copperplate cards, to emphasize the extensive use of this type of engraving in early advertising, not only of trade cards, but noteheads, invoices, tickets of admission, labels, certificates, etc. Well over a hundred years before the advent of the line of wood engravers headed by Alexander Anderson, there were numerous engravers on metal who attacked all manner of problems from the embellishment of fine gold and silver plate to heraldic devices. Henry Pursell announced his readiness (1775) to do "crests . . . doorplates, dog collars, etc." Francis Dewing, arriving from England in 1716, announced: "he likewise cuts neatly and printeth calicoes." And Rollinson is credited with having ornamented the silver buttons on the coat worn by Washington at his inauguration as president. John Conny did Massachusetts bills of credit in 1702-3. Among eighteenth-century engravers of money there was Thomas Sparrow, who did Maryland plates in 1770.

A survey of style in early American trade cards necessarily involves spanning a most significant century—roughly a period from 1750 to 1850. Our Colonial social processes were in a transitory state, older European countries quite naturally setting the pace in matters of cultural interest. So many of the copperplate engravers were either natives of England or leaned so heavily for guidance upon prevailing European styles, that there are no national characteristics in our own handiwork. Lettering on cards follows the school of English calligraphic masters like Bickham, Clark, Bland and Champion. Round hand script and the accompanying flourishes are predominant, interspersed with occasional Roman and Gothic lines. Ornamental designs were fashioned after the somewhat formal, architectonic constructions, including allegorical figures, portrait frames and involved symbolism. Or again, more delicate traceries followed the prevailing vogue for the baroque or the chinoiseries of the Chippendale era. Another group of designs resembled the popular French vignettes, centering around an open cartouche or oval tablet wherein was inscribed the merchant's name and address and a brief description of his offerings. Adele Jenny, in her critical notes introducing the Landauer collection says:

"The earliest examples of American trade cards, on the whole, postulate a fullness of life, a naturalness free from striving, and a fine and honest art. A gradual change to sentimentality and later to 'arty' ideals is noticeable, until out of the exploiting Nineteenth Century there finally came forth again a feeling for art. To apprehend these mutations one need only examine the illustrations on hand."

In consideration of the use of copperplate for our earliest trade cards, antedating Anderson's first use of wood engraving by almost a century, it is well to observe what happened to force it into disuse. Certainly, the medium gave full expression to the artist's imagination, and afforded an excellent vehicle for pictorial representation, engraved lettering, flourishes and embellishments. But copperplate was a form of intaglio engraving that required careful inking, wiping of the plate and printing under pressure at a slow rate, preferably on a good quality rag paper. No suitable method had yet been found for speeding up this process—it remained a costly printing method for more limited presentations.

Wood engraving, on the other hand, a relief printing method, fitted in perfectly with the average printer's requirements. Thus, the early works of Anderson and his contemporaries represented no particular problem. With the advent of the stereotyping process, all these woodcuts could be duplicated and cast in metal in unlimited quantities, resulting in low-priced offerings within the reach of the smallest printshop. It was for this reason that the copperplate was eclipsed and wood engraving became, for the better part of the Nineteenth Century, the most popular and most inexpensive medium for the reproduction of advertising art.

*Typographic design accompanying
early advertising art*

MUCH of the character and temperament of early advertising resides in the typographic accompaniment to the woodcut illustrations. In point of time, the year 1800 marks the approximate beginning of an era that ushered in noteworthy changes in type design. The *modern face,* in contrast to the previously established tradition of the Aldine letter had, throughout Europe, succeeded in supplanting the *oldstyle.* Credit for instituting the break from tradition really belongs to the Scotch founders, Wilson and Fry, who were responsible for developing a very handsome and serviceable letter—the Scotch modern face. The progress of adoption spread rapidly until it included England, Scotland, France and Italy.

Updike, in his scholarly work, *Printing Types,* describes this invention of the modern faces as follows:

"William Blades considered the year 1820 as a boundary line between the old and new style of punchcutting. About that time great changes were initiated in the faces of types of all kinds. The thick strokes were made much thicker and the fine strokes much finer, the old ligatures were abolished and a mechanical primness given to the page, which, artistically, could scarcely be called improvement. At the same time, printers began to crowd their racks with fancy founts of all degrees of grotesqueness, many painfully bad to the eye and unprofitable alike to founder and printer. Thus, taste, which in England had sanctioned very light types, began to change to heavier faces about 1815. Exactly as in France, the weight of these new type faces was at first gained, not by a greater weight of line throughout, but by a disproportionate thickening of heavy strokes of letters, which left their hairlines much as before. This reaction from fragile to sturdy letters was a change which, if it only had been guided by someone familiar with early type forms, might have led to better results. But at that time materials for the comparative study of types were not readily assembled."

The development of the modern face in typography, is all-important for several reasons: it not only signalized the coming of the fat face and its derivatives, but more than that, it represented an emancipation for the type designer, giving him freedom to invent and experiment with new, untried forms. For the first time we recognize a tendency away from purely bookish needs to those of job printing —from a textural type of restraint to bolder, more expressive, more obtrusive forms. The demands of advertising were already making their inroads; the foundries responded with new types to meet these demands. Whatever may be said of these new offerings, they were intended to gain reader attention, not to be beautiful or normal. Updike expresses his contempt most emphatically:

"In London, Robert Thorne, successor to Thomas Cottrell, is responsible for the vilest form of type invented—up to that time. Thorne's specimen book of 'Improved (!) Types' of 1803 should be looked at as a warning of what fashion can make men do. His 'jobbing types' look as their name suggests! His black-letter is perhaps the worst that ever appeared in England. In Vincent Figgins' specimen of 1815 and in Fry's specimen of 1816, and naturally in the specimen of William Thorowgood (Thorne's successor) of 1824, 1832, and 1837, the new styles are triumphant. Fashions like these, as Hansard says, 'have left the specimens of a British letter founder a heterogeneous compound, made up of fat faces and lean faces, wide-set and close-set, all at once crying *Quosque tandem abutere, Catilina, patientia nostra?*' "

The most detailed account of the varying type styles of the early Nineteenth Century, especially as they foreshadow the evolution into advertising display faces, is given in a volume by Nicolette Gray, called *Nineteenth Century Ornamented Types and Title Pages.* Realizing the importance of the fat face as a basis for subsequent development, Gray dwells at considerable length on the original forms:

"The fat face is usually considered to be a swollen version of the modern face. If we are to accept this account, it is necessary to modify Mr. A. F. Johnson's definition of the characteristics of modern face as (a) flat and unbracketed serifs, (b) abrupt and exaggerated modeling, (c) vertical shading. These characteristics apply to modern face regarded as a book type (as it essentially is), and are based on the design of the lower case.

"I (Nicolette Gray) should define the fully developed fat face as a large letter with (a) vertical shading, (b) abrupt modeling, so exaggerated that the thick stroke is nearly half as wide as the letter is high, and (c) certain characteristic forms, all tending to emphasize roundness in the letters; R with a curly tail, short ranging J terminating in a round blob, Q with a tail making a loop within the bowl, S, C and G with barbed terminals and G with a pointed spur. These letter forms are found in all the original fat face designs; they are also characteristic of modern face design, but are not found in book faces with anything of the same uniformity. The serifs of the fat face may be unbracketed or slightly bracketed, but those terminating in a thin vertical stroke are always bracketed."

While the origins of the fat face are obscure, it is nevertheless clear that they developed, as an advertising expediency, from normal letters accentuated to grotesque proportions. Their earliest applications have been traced in England by A. F. Johnson to lottery tickets and bills and theatrical posters. The needs for a purely functional change from existing styles produced a quite natural heavy letter, immediately seized upon by founders throughout the British realm. Instead of the weak lines

and thin serifs of the fat face, here are "magnificent solid stems founded on serifs like rocks. All the colour and emphasis is retained without that suggestion of insufficient support to its grandeur which is the weakness of the first display type. . . . The founders succeeded in mastering the principles of the upper case letter with amazing skill, noticeably different from their clumsy control of the sans serif when it first became popular."

Gray, in her admirable study of type evolution, continues with these comments on the prevailing trends:

"It is in this period that the vista opened by the revolution in typographical purpose is first explored. If the purpose of a letter is to be expressive, it follows that its differentiations may be in infinite variety. Between 1810 and 1815 were developed not only the two principles for the variation of lettering, by modification of the form and by decoration of the face, but also that idea which enormously enriched the possibilities under either principle, that of the three dimensional letter.

"The first shadowed letters (1815) are characteristic and distinct from all the hundreds of letters to follow." (The *Thorne Shaded* brought out in 1936 by Stephenson Blake is a revival of a Regency type.) "Here again the founders seem to be providing compensation for the thin stems and hair serifs of the fat face; they seem to have been very conscious of its inadequacy. The appeal of the obvious illusion is hard to explain, or to deny. These faces, light, yet square and solid, are enjoyable without being particularly characteristic of either a mood or a period. It is as if the designers were absorbed in enjoying the ingenuity of their own invention. The introduction was immediately popular. Every founder came out in a wide range of sizes, many with italic. The variation in the width of the shadow was considerable. A significant point is the introduction of quite small sizes, and it is remarkable how the letter changes with its size. The big letter is very full and bulky, very near to its parent fat face. The small letter is almost elegant, far nearer to the succeeding outline types.

"The first ornamented types are rather dull and clumsy; they are important as technical innovations, but the designers have not yet sufficient mastery of their new medium to enable them to use it with sophistication. They were also no doubt hampered by technical difficulties in casting."

SPECIAL FEATURE ISSUES OF EARLY AMERICAN NEWSPAPERS

The Peace edition of the Albany Argus, Feb. 21, 1815 and the George Washington centennial edition of the Philadelphia Chronicle, Feb. 22, 1832, both use wood engravings to brighten important news announcements. *N. Y. Historical Society.*

Another distinct addition to the type family of the early Nineteenth Century is a pronounced fat-faced version of Gothic—a black letter which soon made the rounds of the American foundries after a popular reception abroad. Gothics had fallen into a state of disuse, but with the prevalent style of architecture in England and its subsequent importation into this country, the Gothic revival meant "the gothicising of country seats and the building of sham castles."

The new black letter, as described by a contemporary writer, "transforms the stately magnificence of the Gothic letter into something fantastically flamboyant." The applications were many, particularly in handbills and posters of stage lines, railroads, shipping schedules and announcements. The larger sizes and the highlighted version of the text letter made it desirable for the giant broadsides that became more numerous in the thirties and forties.

In this same period, still another important letter design emerges from the revivalism of the English regency—a type at first called Antique, but later known popularly by its alternative name, Egyptian. It was so called undoubtedly because of its "darkness," and the current interest in the archeological discoveries along the Nile. Its chief characteristics are an evenness of line and heavy slab serifs—a swollen type form in which both "hairlines" and stems are of nearly equal weight (known today by its twentieth-century counterparts in type under the names Beton, Memphis and Girder). Nicolette Gray says:

"The Egyptian is, I think, the most brilliant typographical invention of the century, and perhaps the most complete and concise expression of the dominant culture of its brief period; more inspired than contemporary paintings, combining the elegance of the furniture, and weight of the architecture, and the colour and precise romance of Bulwer Lytton.

". . . Instead of the weak lines and thin serifs of the fat face, here are magnificent solid stems founded on serifs like rocks. All the colour and emphasis is retained without that suggestion of insufficient support to its grandeur which is the weakness of the first display type. The difficulty of making terminals to the arms of T and E which shall be firm enough without being too curved or too pointed is overcome by the neat yet solid slab, while the very short ascenders and descenders of the lower case make the type wonderfully terse and compact."

Now while all the foregoing discussion about new typographical fashions relates to conditions to be met with in England, it is amazingly true of American type display as well—with but one major exception. The inventions and innovations at this step were entirely a matter for the British and Scotch founders and designers; American founders merely awaited the arrival of each new specimen or type from abroad, and imitated it without change or variation. Comparison between specimen showings on both sides of the Atlantic told to what degree we were still tied by the umbilical cord to Europe's more mature culture of centuries.

It may be with considerable generosity that we attribute this status entirely to unpreparedness. There is involved a vastly more important principle of ethics casting its shadow over type founding practices both here and abroad, and exposing all operations to question and scrutiny. It is certainly not a matter of mere coincidence that we find, on comparing the offerings of contemporary foundries, a striking parallel in the faces issued. The pattern of resemblances is too strongly outlined to be dismissed lightly; the process follows along these lines: a type founder would pioneer in the development of a new style of face, followed by its issuance in specimen showings. In time, the new style met with some measure of success. Before several years had elapsed, other competitive foundries started producing the exact letter, making certain, however, that a safe probationary period had passed during which a sustained demand was established. In rapid succession, the remaining foundries repeated the process until fin-

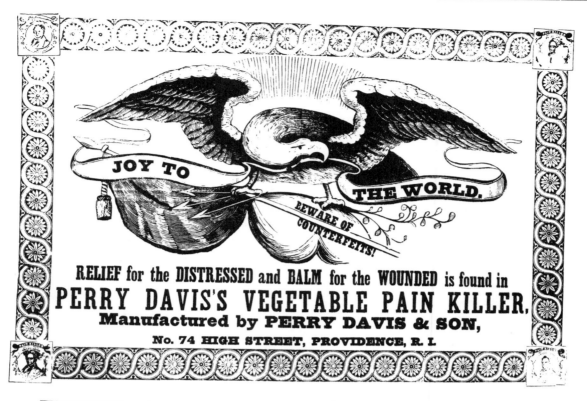

POSTERS FOR PATENT MEDICINE AND LOTTERY DRAWING

Manufacturers of patent medicines were among the largest and most consistent advertisers in the early 1800's. When in doubt for a central theme, the advertiser could always rely upon the popularity of the American eagle. In the lottery poster which was printed on linen, in 1832, the engraving shows a particularly spirited handling of the crowds in attendance. *Courtesy American Antiquarian Society & N. Y. Public Library.*

ally, the "new style" was fully accepted and adopted—all this with little or no change in the original conception of the letter.

For a brief and poignant summary of the type and woodcut characteristics of this period, here are the words of Edmund Gress speaking in his *Fashions in American Typography:*

"The panel of type faces presents those letters typical of 1840: the italic of extreme contrast of strokes, with the ball finishing off the serifs, the so-called text letter with thin shading line, the Roman letter of contrasted strokes, the outline letter with black shading, the so-called 'Antique' type of heavy lines of the same width, the light face Roman, the black Antique type face with hairline shading, the condensed Antique letter, the black Antique letter with an outer hairline following the contour of the type face, and the extra condensed Roman and the expanded Roman with great contrast of color.

"A study of the type faces and woodcuts of the period reveals that they 'belong.' There is a dominant black tone in the types. and in the illustrations, combined with certain squareness and plainness of form, that reflects a rugged and pioneering mood: log cabins, canal boats, black plug hats, black boots, stages, covered wagons, black beards, masted schooners and storms at sea, black frock coats of southern gentlemen, black smoke from the funnels of the new steamers. It was a period of strength of character and purpose."

PART 6

Period from 1840 to 1865 witnesses development of new advertising forms

THE tremendous expansion of manufacturing and distribution facilities which was a feature of American national life in the years following the end of the Civil War made the quick business promotion afforded by advertising indispensable for the health of our growing industrial economy. New manufacturers discovered the bonanza powers of advertising, while some of the old line merchants and makers were introduced to its advantages for the first time. The canal and stage lines, the river boats and railroads all had important announcements to make or schedules to place before the public. Newspapers, naturally, constituted the principal advertising medium for such announcements, and enjoyed an unprecedented period of prosperity during these days of heavy expansion. In 1847, about eleven million separate advertisements, mostly small insertions, were placed in some two thousand American newspapers. Frank Presbrey in his *History and Development of Advertising* describes these as follows:

"One day the iconoclastic *Herald* appeared with a paid sensation. The advertisement not only was set two columns wide, but had a double column illustration, a fire scene depicting the 'Unparalleled Attraction at the American Museum,' namely 'Harrington's New Grand Moving Deorance, Showing the Awful and Devastating Conflagration of a Large Part of the City of New York on the inclement night of the 10th of December, 1835, and ensuing days.' Thereafter a limited number of two column advertisements appeared in the New York papers for a time. A striking one noted in the *New York Evening Post* in 1838 carried a two column cut of the British royal arms. It advised the use of Cullen's Prophylactic Pills. In the *Herald* these two column advertisements would run from ten to forty lines in depth and sometimes three or four of them would appear the same day, always over or under others of the same width, and never scattered in the paper. Pianos, shaving cream and cooking stoves were among the articles for which double column width

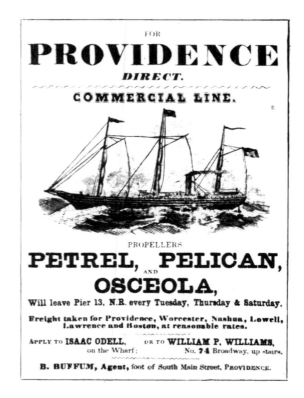

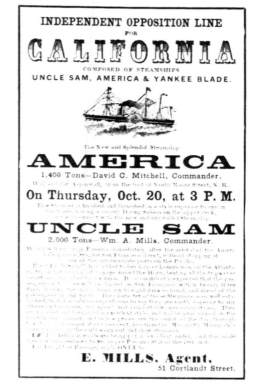

SHIPPING POSTERS OF THE MIDDLE NINETEENTH CENTURY

Sailing announcements followed a well-established pattern with destination listed at top, followed by a wood engraving of the vessel, its name and other details set below in smaller type. Printers in shipping ports carried stock cuts of many types of sailing vessels. *Landauer Collection.*

was used in 1840. In the luxury class the piano and organ are, incidentally, our oldest advertisers.

"Probably the largest piece of newspaper advertising copy that appeared in this brief period of display was a machinery advertisement. It measured twelve inches on three columns and was set in 8-point type across the three columns, with a 14-point caption. It doubtless started as a handbill. The subject was Hardy and Roche's Self-Setting Saw Mill Dogs, the manufacturers of which were 'confident they need only name the positive advantages which are to be derived from their use to induce every owner of a saw mill to cause a set to be immediately placed in his mill.' The advertisement concluded with what a twentieth-century advertising man would regard as a naïve suggestion: 'Persons receiving this advertisement will please cut it out of the paper and put it securely in Mills, Stores and their Hotels.'"

In spite of a few attempts by outstanding individual advertisers, the general tenor of newspaper insertions was monotonously dull. Many regular small space users complained that the bizarre effects of a few diverted attention from their messages, and so threatened to withdraw. The *Herald*, in 1847, announced that it would ban all display ads including cuts of any real size. Most other papers followed suit, although in Boston and Philadelphia merchants were encouraged to use display type and column-wide illustrations. Want-ad styles prevailed, in page upon page of newspaper columns, the only note of relief being provided by small fingernail stereotype cuts such as those to be found in early eighteenth-century advertising. The foundries, in order to meet this demand for minimum sized cuts, produced hundreds of new designs which were featured in their catalogs as "newspaper cuts." But the absence of larger illustrations hurt the publishers who were trying to find a solution to an unhappy situation. The setback in advertising art at a time when the nation was entering one of the most promising eras in history struck a sour note; fortunately, however, it was of short duration.

Where the newspapers, in their momentary decline in influence, failed to afford opportunities to the advertiser, other media stepped in to fill the gap. Outdoor forms of advertising became attractive, especially to advertisers who sought a "wallop" in their messages. Hand-painted signs on rocks and brick walls appeared in the cities. Merchants' names and products were emblazoned in huge letters, sometimes covering an entire building, as seen in early prints of streets in lower New York. Busy thoroughfares like Broadway and the Bowery and main streets of the more populous cities were often a mass of signs and streamers. "Sandwich men," carrying their portable displays, had appeared on lower Broadway as early as the 1820's, and wagons bearing banners and pennants were introduced in New York in 1830. This type of blatant advertising with its attendant ballyhoo and circus stunts was carried to the zenith of perfection by Phineas T. Barnum, one of the greatest exploiters of stunt publicity the world has ever known. His influence did much to stimulate advertising methods and carry it away from its lethargy of conservatism. Results proved beyond all doubt that fanfare and extremism could be successfully harnessed into the advertising schemes of certain types of products.

Barnum's first advertising efforts were applied to selling lottery tickets in his home town of Bethel, Connecticut. Here, he used handbills and circulars written in extravagant language, printed with bold, startling display effects—the most garish that the local printer had to offer. He employed immense gold signs and lurid posters, hired brass bands and thought up parades on the slightest provocation. Barnum was undoubtedly influenced by the notable success of patent medicine makers, who for a century, had found that extravagant claims and unrestrained statements in their advertising paid off in handsome profits. While Barnum was not the originator of this type of display, he, more than any other single individual, perfected its technique. His superlative showmanship gave a

A LEADING MERCHANT'S FULL PAGE IN DIRECTORY, 1854

The Illustrated American Biography was a popular, sumptuous annual containing hundreds of pages of advertisements of stores, publishers, manufacturers, hotels and resorts throughout the eastern United States.

new impetus and meaning to the sense of the colossal, and in so doing made all advertisers conscious of a thunder-and-lightning approach hitherto neglected.

The existing media open to the advertiser were widely extended during this period. In many instances these were the more mature developments of efforts inaugurated in earlier years; in others, they were new ventures in fields hitherto unexplored. The publication of city directories had, of course, become an established enterprise at the turn of the century. As the cities grew and prospered, their annual volumes became stouter with each new issue. As other cities developed into importance and the neighboring environs were extended, new town and county directories appeared. Each year, as conditions warranted, new names and addresses were added, new editorial features were introduced, and above all, new advertisers who had never before appeared between the covers of a book, were lured into the advertising pages.

The order of the city directory pages followed a simple pattern: an historical sketch of the community from its founding with some very rosy promise as to its future growth, a description of important buildings and places of interest, a listing of town officers and councilmen, police and fire departments, schools, hospitals and institutions, an alphabetical index of all inhabitants with their occupation (often with a separate appendix listing "inhabitants of color"), followed by a section either in the rear or (sometimes) the front of the book containing the ads of the more progressive merchants and tradesmen. In the early volumes, there was no clearly defined section; the ads were scattered like so many "cards" throughout the pages.

Such advertisements offer the best available study we have of the character of prevailing advertising design. The cuts at the top of each ad were usually selected by the printer from his collection of stock material supplied by the type foundries in our leading cities. The most useful of these illustrations were known as "business or trade cuts" and included pictures and decorative compositions emblematic of furniture, jewelry, grocery, hardware, wagon works, lumber supplies, the wheelwright, the confectioner, the baker and a host of other trades and services sufficient to cover every possible type of business in the community. The ads were set in simple directory style, with little to differentiate between "cards" of competitive advertisers. This matter of display presented many problems since there were bound to be repetitions more numerous than could be handled effectively by the stock cuts. To overcome this condition the printer would order several sets of business cards from different foundries to enlarge his assortment, enabling him to solicit advertising from many more merchants in town. Thus, a directory might contain the ads of a dozen grocers or undertakers, and if the printer's equipment was adequate, he did not incur the displeasure of his advertisers with repeated cuts. Early in the course of directory printing, someone hit upon another very ingenious expedient—the use of colored papers scattered throughout the advertising section. With a half-dozen delightful gay tints, light blue, pink, cream, yellow, orange and lavender, he could imbue his pages with a sparkling note of gaiety adding life to the book while diverting attention from whatever lack of variety his cases afforded.

The success that attended the publication of various directories soon gave rise to a new type of volume designed to attract advertising revenue. Notable in the new order was a series of books first published in New York in 1853, called *The Illustrated American Biography*. Six volumes were issued on an annual basis, described in the book's elaborate title as "containing correct portraits and brief notices of the principal actors in American history; embracing distinguished women, naval and military heroes, statesmen, civilians, jurists, divines, authors, and artists; together

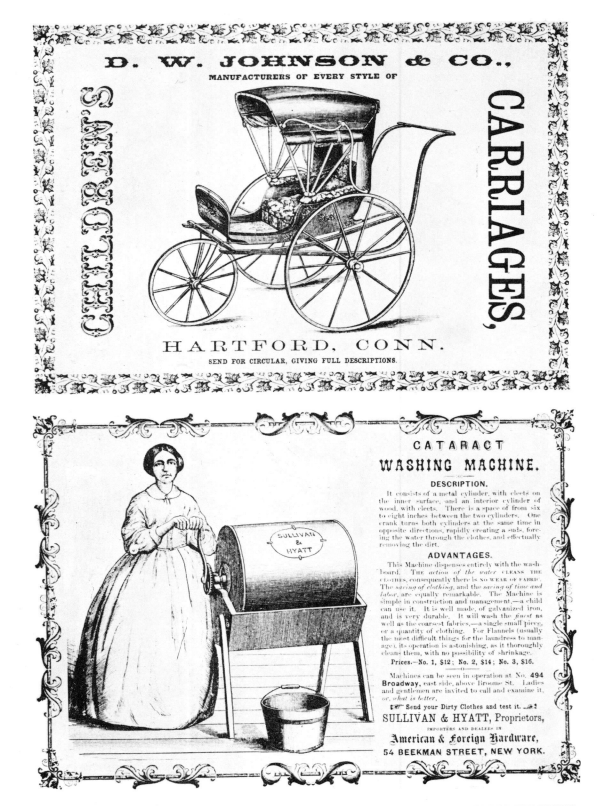

ADVERTISING VOLUMES AFFORD RARE DISPLAY OPPORTUNITIES

While newspapers of this era generally banned prominent illustrations, the new advertising books offered special inducements to advertisers desirous of showing their products, shopfronts and industrial establishments. The washing machine cut of the early 50's is one of the first of its kind.

with celebrated Indian chiefs from Christopher Columbus down to the present time." Nothing can quite compare with the simple, frank statement of the publishers, J. M. Emerson and A. D. Jones who address the readers as follows:

"To Our Patrons. It is a desideratum in advertising to combine economy with attractiveness—to present the advertisements in conjunction with something which will attract the attention, not only of the commercial community, but also of such persons of taste as are looking for the beautiful and intellectual as well as the useful. This combination we think we have happily effected; and we trust that the present volume, which is the first of a series of six, to appear annually, will approve itself to our advertising patrons, and induce them to continue the very liberal encouragement bestowed thus far upon our efforts. Alternating, as they do, with the portraits and biographies, every advertisement comes directly under the eye of the reader, and cannot fail to arrest his attention; and hundreds of persons, who are spending an idle hour at their hotel, or a wearisome one on board a steamer, may be attracted to an advertisement which might have entirely escaped their attention in the ordinary modes of such communications."

To better understand the success of the many new advertising volumes that appeared, it should be remembered that at this time there also appeared countless illustrated books and gift volumes whose popularity helped pave the way for related items. These "literary annuals" had, by the middle of the century, reached such proportions that no parlor living room was completely furnished unless one of these sumptuous tomes, gaudily gold stamped, with pin grain morocco or silken brocade binding, reposed on the library table. It had become quite the fashion for gentlemen and ladies to exchange these sentimental collections. Their literary contents included an assortment of odd selections of poetry, bits of witticism, essays, biographies and the favorite sentiments of the day. Their format varied greatly, reflecting the many prevailing techniques of illustration: copperplate, steel engraving, chromolithography, mezzotint and wood engraving.

The typographic style of the advertising pages of these volumes followed closely an accepted pattern. Since full pages became the rule, it was simple to adopt a unified scheme consisting of three main elements. Dominating the page, invariably placed near the top, was a single illustration executed in wood engraving. Below this followed a dozen or more display lines set in a wide assortment of decorative and fanciful styles. All lines were centered; no two were alike in size or style. Surrounding the entire ad was a border composed of printer's flowers, often very ornate. The foundry catalog was replete with a wide variety of these offerings, mostly elaborate in the current decorative tradition.

The display types with which the compositor set his advertisements ran the gamut of wild extravagance and virtuosity, and yet there was an underlying unity to this period, typographically speaking. The romanticism and mysticism of the forties and fifties greatly influenced the decorated letter forms, compressed and squeezed them into a state of pronounced perpendicularity. The hairline serifs were then twisted and curled into scrolled volutes; or the squared terminations of the Egyptians, Ionics and Antiques were given an extra heavy emphasis. Throughout these pained mutations, there was evident the strong influence of the prevailing Gothic revival, manifest not only in the architectural mood imported from Europe, but in the literary and scholarly tendencies of the day. The Gothic style became an escape for all forms of intellectual imagination. It provided a new language of expression for the early Victorians, who now began to cultivate the remnants of medieval romance. According to Nicolette Gray:

"It was in the forties that the demand which has culminated in surrealism became urgent. Now for the first time fairy stories were popular; nursery rhymes, fairy tales and remnants of the medieval romances have had a continuous oral tradition; many were printed as chapbooks and sold among the people for a few pence, but the universal acceptance of tales of

BARTLETT BENT, JR.,

129

No. 238 Water Street, New York,

Manufacturer and Dealer in

STOVES,

Of every Variety and most Fashionable Patterns.

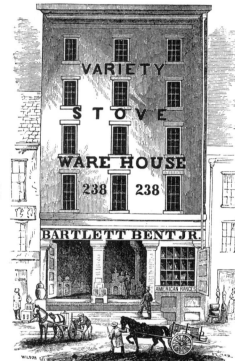

PARLOR GRATES	FARMERS' BOILERS
AND	OR
FENDERS,	CAULDRON
OF	FURNACES
LATEST STYLE	FOR
AND	Agricultural
Originality	OR
OF	LAUNDRY
DESIGN.	PURPOSES.

SOLE AGENT FOR A. C. TAYLOR & CO.'S

IMPROVED PORTABLE FORGE AND BELLOWS.

BARTLETT BENT, JR.,

238 WATER STREET, NEW YORK.

VARIETY OF TYPE STYLES A FEATURE OF MOST ADS

Frequently the advertisement resembled a printer's specimen sheet in which he demonstrated the great number of faces at his disposal. Emphasis is often wrongly placed, as in the name and address at the bottom.

wonder as respectable and necessary children's literature was not till the forties."

The full flowering of mid-nineteenth-century advertising style was in no small measure due to the unrestrained outpourings of the type foundries. Of their illustrations and decorative pieces, much has already been said—now let us turn to examine the prolific character of display faces and type styles. The decade preceding the year 1850 was a particularly active one; in it, we see the merging of the inventive genius of the letter designer, not as an individual of established repute and recognition, but as an adjunct of the art staff of the foundry, serving anonymously. Type offerings seemed to flow on in endless succession, with hundreds of different varieties of letters that beggar description and classification. Basically, however, they may be placed into three main groupings: one, those letters whose shapes assume new forms and outlines, varying from simpler to more embroidered types; second, three-dimensional letters, whose depth and relief is made to vary with strength and blackness of shadow; and third, letters that have been designed into some form of background, network or ribbon arrangement. Of all these multitudinous designs, none so identifies the period of the "Roaring Forties" as the shadow or relief letter. The flair for the creation of three-dimensional styles resulted in light shadows and heavy ones, some that preceded and others that followed the letter. We find ominous black shadows, and grained or stippled shadows or airy, gray texture. As for the body of these letters, imagination runs riot and includes zebra-like stripings, intricate scale patterns and those imitative of special materials such as stone, metal, masonry and rustic log effects. And finally there are those predominantly black ribbon and band style letters cut out in reverse. They seem to have sprung full-grown in this era, tracing their distant origins to both England and Germany where they appeared from 1836 to 1841. Sometimes these white letters are mounted on backgrounds with vertical palings or picket effects. Other effects include architectural brickwork, bejewelled incrustations and hairline traceries in varying degrees of light and shade.

After the introduction of the above-named styles, the types born of the fifties seem to show a complete reversal in mood. The wild, experimental spirit of the previous decade gave way to a more sobering influence, bringing in its wake a line of more legible faces. The fanciful letters and soaring perpendiculars disappear from the specimen books, to be replaced by more practical, medium-sized letters stripped of most excrescences. The sans serif was just emerging from its chrysallis, setting the style and symbolizing the reactions of the Victorian era.

In the handbills of auction and slave sales, railroad schedules and steamer sailings, as well as political broadsides and recruiting posters, one can observe how display lines were losing the bizarre extravagance that characterized earlier efforts. It was as if the slowly increasing trend of mechanization was restoring some sanity in the midst of chaos. The influence of railways, suspension bridges and cast-iron construction brought forth an age of prosperity and good living; at the same time, it produced an aesthetic realization of the values of simpler forms, a first introductory taste and appreciation of functionalism in design. It is interesting, in this connection, that the sans serif letter which we, in the Twentieth Century, have regarded as a product of our Twenties and symbol of this day, was really the high-water mark of the period of the 1850's.

No discussion of this period would be complete unless attention were called to the influence upon the advertising arts of the growth of the nationalist spirit. A large proportion of the illustrations appearing at about the half-way mark of the Nineteenth Century and continuing, through the Civil War era, both as newspaper cuts and broadsides decorations,

If Martin Van Buren is elected President, Connecticut will not receive any of the Surplus Revenue—He is opposed to the distribution among the people—He has said so! Connecticut will lose her share of

50,000,000 !

Nearly $5 to every Man, Woman and Child in the State.

VOTE FOR

HARRISON,
AND DIVIDE THE
SURPLUS.

☞ *See to it in time—NOW or NEVER!*

HUZZAH FOR

Wm. H. Harrison!

REPUBLICAN TICKET.

For Governor,
Ichabod Goodwin

For Railroad Commissioner,   JEREMIAH C. TILTON.
REED P. CLARK, Councillor.
CLEMENT MARCH, Senator.
SAMUEL A. HALEY, Treasurer.
ALONZO J. FOGG, Register.
FRANKLIN CROMBIE, Commissioner.

Theodore W. Frost, Representative

TO ARMS!

CITIZENS OF HEMPSTEAD AND NORTH HEMPSTEAD,
DO YOU HEAR THE CALL OF YOUR COUNTRY, BECKONING YOU TO ARMS?

BY THE FOLLOWING ORDER--

Special Orders to wit :l2b: CAPT. WILLIS, 119th Reg't N. Y. V. is detailed on the Recruiting service, and will report for instructions to the Superintendent of the Recruiting Service of the State of New York.
By Command of MAJOR-GENERAL McCLELLAN.
RICH'D B. IRWIN, CAPT. A. D. C. A. A. G.

I am with you again, but a few days only! I want to take back with me to Washington 100 MEN! They must be had in six days! The hour is at hand! Fellow-Citizens, will you Respond? Your proud past speaks for you.

Show your Countrymen that you choose Honor and Glory before humiliation and shame. Let every man attend a

Grand Mass Meeting
TO BE HELD AT HEMPSTEAD,
WEDNESDAY, SEPT. 17, '62,
AT HEWLETT'S HOTEL,
AT HALF-PAST SEVEN O'CLOCK P. M.

☞ Citizens, prove yourselves worthy of the 19th Century.

BENJ. A. WILLIS,
Capt. Co. H, 119th Reg't N. Y.

BAKER & GODWIN, Printers, Printing-House Square, opposite City Hall, N. Y.

FALL IN! FALL IN! FALL IN!
Senatorial Regiment
COLONEL ANTHONY CONK.

RECRUITS WANTED
To fill up a Company of this Regiment, under the command of Officers who have seen service in the field.

The following Bounties will be paid to all those who volunteer:

The City of Brooklyn, ... $60
The State, ... 50
The United States, ... 102
One Month's Pay in Advance, ... 13

☞ **$225** ☜

$150 before leaving the State, and $75 as soon as discharged!

PAY commences from date of enlistment, and good QUARTERS and RATIONS provided immediately.

CAPT. J. W. SWIFT,
1st LIEUT. E. ROGERS,   Recruiting Officers.

Tent, City Hall Park, Brooklyn.

BAKER & GODWIN, Printers, Printing-House Square, opposite City Hall, N. Y.

GROWING NATIONALISM EVIDENT IN USE OF PATRIOTIC EMBLEMS

The two top posters show the same eagle cut, the left printed during the bitter Whig campaign of 1840 and the one at the right appearing in 1860. Of the many hundreds of Civil War recruiting posters, seldom is the eagle omitted from northern posters. Larger size permitted special emblems to be engraved for the occasion.

bear the stamp of their time—an unmistakable economy of line and simplicity in composition, coupled with subject matter strongly characteristic of national feelings.

The Erie Canal . . . the rise of the clippers . . . the growth of the railroads . . .Texas . . . the gold rush . . . these are but a few highlights of the intense growth and expansion. Side by side with the acquisition of new lands came mechanical improvements and material development. The nation was bursting at its boundaries with each generation, pulsating, seething, shouting aloud to the world to match its newfound strength.

Throughout this entire period, nothing is quite so striking as the continuous repetition of popular emblems and patriotic motifs. Eagles are to be found everywhere—their different attitudes exhibit a vitality of expression that is amazing. Anderson, the early wood engraver, at the height of his career, must have accounted for many hundreds of eagle engravings, as his elaborate scrapbooks plainly show. All of this early work is particularly distinguished by an honest craftsman's feeling for construction, simplicity and just proportion. Springing from the heart of folk experience, these efforts concentrate the meanings of democratic tradition; their repeated use only emphasize that the eagle had become an exponent of unity and freedom, and had initiated the creative forces at work in American society. It marked the beginnings of important social and economic influences, the process of promoting advertised brands— the voice of the people that seemed glad to shout out: "Made in U.S.A."

The use of the eagle in printing and advertising grew rapidly with the expansion of the country in the first half of the Nineteenth Century. Likenesses of American heroes such as General Zachary Taylor, "Old Rough and Ready" of Mexican War fame, and William Henry Harrison, the hero of Tippecanoe, were always accompanied by eagle ornaments in appropriate settings, whether printed or en-

graved. During troublesome Civil War days, besides its extensive use on military equipment and household accessories, the eagle was broadly used on ballots, handbills, broadsides and especially on recruiting posters. Printers invariably set these messages in large type, surmounted at the top of the sheet with one of a number of typical poses of fighting eagles screaming their battle cries of freedom: "The Nation, one and inseparable," "In Union there is strength," "Constitution and Country."

Post Civil War and Centennial era sees wide expansion in use of illustration—while taste declines

THE Civil War decade witnessed a number of far-reaching developments in the technique of advertising. The hunger for war news boosted the circulation of daily newspapers to unprecedented proportions, and led to special Sunday editions— a new departure in the American press. A vastly wider circulation for the advertiser's message was thus assured, a factor that not only stimulated the growth of linage of old line advertisers, but, what was even more important, attracted many new ones as well. Thus, the skeptical and timid merchants and manufacturers were brought into line, and the position of advertising was more firmly entrenched in the general scheme of business.

Wartime shortages in material spurred

activities looking towards improvements in printing and publishing. The advent of pulp paper and the introduction of the curved stereotype plate did much to revolutionize newspaper printing. In 1865 a new cylinder press was perfected by William Bullock. This machine, printing a large newspaper on both sides of a continuous web of newsprint, enabled the newspaper publisher to print ten thousand copies an hour without the assistance of feeders. This was regarded as a great advance, but some defects had yet to be solved in the neat folding of the papers. Not until R. Hoe and Company produced the web press in 1871, was this fully and successfully accomplished. Coincident with the deep-seated changes in industrial processes came certain corollary sociological ones—especially the growing importance of women as factors in purchasing. It had been the established custom for men to do the family shopping at the general store, grain and feed shop or in the large emporia in the metropolitan centers. The war had served to release many women from their household tasks to take on the duties and responsibilities of running the newborn machines. The family purchases ceased to be man's exclusive domain; henceforth, as her visits to the shopping centers became a regular habit, woman's influence was dominant. The shopkeeper, the merchant and manufacturer, and the advertiser made necessary adjustments in their consumer calculations.

It was to be expected that, in the wake of this important shift and the growing interests of milady, new publications would arise catering exclusively to women. Such magazines were slow in starting, but once launched, took hold and grew at a rapid pace. Most typical of the day, though well established at a much earlier date, was Godey's Lady's Book, "A Magazine of Belles Lettres, Fashions, Music, etc." It employed steel engravings and color to depict the new styles as they appeared, and has become an invaluable record of the modes and manners of the times. Godey's circulation reached 65,000 in the 1850's and over 100,000 in the sixties. Peterson's, a competitive magazine, reached 140,000 in 1869. Advertising was decidedly scant in these publications, reflecting a limitation current at the time, but a definite foothold was established that later was to blossom forth into many charming periodicals.

From the standpoint of their influence upon the face of advertising art, the most significant publications of this period were the pictorials. There was Gleason's Pictorial Drawing Room Companion, 11" by 15" in page size, published in Boston. Harper's Weekly, born in 1857, started its life as a literary vehicle, but with the coming of the war it became the leading news-picture periodical. Leslie's Weekly was started in 1852 by Frank Leslie, one of Gleason's wood engravers. All enjoyed tremendous sales during the war years and thereafter. They employed a large staff of engravers, many of whom were sent to the front to do pictorial sketching. Thomas Nast, who later became one of America's greatest cartoonists and propagandists, was employed by Harper's to sketch war scenes. As these weeklies developed engravers, their influence spread into the advertising columns. This available art talent meant that the advertiser was no longer limited to stock cuts and the products of the meagre handful of original engravers; a lively competition ensued, with the more successful of the engravers building up a large clientele and in some cases, a sizable staff of assistants.

While the medium of lithography plays a comparatively minor role in the development of early American advertising, its part is, nevertheless, a peculiar specialty that merits attention. In 1819 a painter named Bass Otis first used the grease crayon technique in the rendition of two landscape prints. His efforts were quite unimportant except in point of priority, and gave little promise of the commercial possibilties that were to develop within the next fifty years. Here and there in the major cities professional lithographic artists soon appeared, some doing portrait work and genre scenes, others specializing in scenic views of all descriptions. Included in the list of artists were such names as Moses Sweett, R. Cooke, P. S. Duval, C. W. Burton, F. J. Fritsch, Charles Gildemeister, Albert Newsam, Childs & Inman, Peter Maverick, etc.

Among the many popular prints that were produced and published by individuals and firms such as Annin & Smith, W. S. Pendleton, F. & S. Palmer and Currier & Ives were sets of views featuring both city and country. Those that interest us, since they fall into a very special category of advertising ephemera, were the metropolitan street scenes like the series published in New York by William Stephenson, 1854 to 1873. These prints contain the germ of a new advertising thought because they depicted merchants' building façades in which particular emphasis was placed on the signs above the storefronts and buildings. The Stephenson views, totaling nineteen in number, varied in size, the largest measuring about 37" long by 17" high. Thomas Hamilton Ormsbee, commenting on these publicity prints in his article "Advertising Prints a Phase of American Lithography" says:

"The record of American development would be incomplete without the lithographic advertising prints of the Nineteenth Century. Although originally published to be given away by the company or businessman whose name they bore, they are not of inferior work and, in some instances, are the only pictorial records of their kind. There was a good reason for these advertising lithographs which bear the imprint of all of the outstanding print makers. Newspapers and other publications of the day would not break their column rules to allow an advertiser to illustrate his copy with anything larger than crude wood cuts or engravings on copper, which measured about two inches in width."

Still further comment on these prints appears in the Bulletin of the Museum of the City of New York as follows: "Since the Stephenson Views are not devoted to the advertisement of a single product or concern, it is believed that all the tenants of a given block were canvassed, and invited to pay for the dear privilege of having their signs appear on the façades of the buildings they occupied. Failure to contribute resulted in a complete 'black-out' or anonymity. This theory is further substantiated by an earlier G. & W. Endicott lithograph of 'The Washington Stores,' as the impression owned by the Museum bears the pencilled notations, probably indicating the amount each firm was taxed, fifty-five cents per $100 (rent or cost of production?) being the price of glory."

Immediately following the Civil War the field of lithography began to show rapid progress as it applied its talents to serving commerce and industry. With the development of color lithography, individual artists and commercial partnerships were kept busy supplying the demands for trade cards, cigar box labels, music sheet covers, Christmas designs, calendars, book illustrations, advertisements, periodical supplements, fashion plates and billboard posters. The greatest strides were made in the department of outdoor advertising. Starting abroad in 1867, largely through the efforts of a French perfume label designer, Jules Cheret, the development of the poster soon spread to this country, where it found expression in billboards and circus announcements, ship sailings and posters for patent medicines. But the litho print had to fight its way against strong opposition. The printer, through his use of large woodcut blocks, was able, by virtue of more economical means of securing bold effects, to offer real competition. He had a liberal assortment of giant wood letters made available by the foundries and engraving houses, which, when combined with stock emblems or specially engraved pictures, succeeded for all purposes. Not until the more mature development of chromolithography and the unsurpassed facsimile effects made possible by the new process, did this medium finally outstrip the printer's crude woodcut and typographic offerings, and then only for very special jobs and the larger runs.

The advent of lithography and its progressive flowering into forms more colorful and more elaborately embellished than had previously been known established correspond-

BOOK PAGE OF ONE OF AMERICA'S OLDEST ADVERTISERS

This is typical of many involved, allegorical decorations featured in advertisements during the latter half of the Nineteenth Century. Lettering, decoration and picture are blended en masse, with no attempt at legibility or advertising message.

ingly new canons of bad taste. The "artistic" race between printer and lithographer came at a time when postwar conditions favored extravagance and excesses in all directions, and now more than ever, the time appeared ripe for the bombastic, distorted and over-ornamental type faces and their pictorial accompaniments. Sanity and restraint were discarded to the four winds as advertising pages became a riot of confusion. The compositor, playing his part with gusto and egotism, employed at least a dozen type styles in every page. He suddenly became the virtuoso who controlled the appearance of the printed page, subjugating the role of both illustrator and engraver and calling the tunes of letter designer and type founder as well. Nowhere is the story of this notable decline in taste so admirably described and so vehemently denounced as in the following description by A. J. Corrigan, of England, in his book *A Printer and His World:*

"Instantly we except the artists here. There were and there are artists on stone and plate whose lettering is an abiding joy, and the despair of the typographic craftsman. They are free of our question and our criticism alike; they denounce more strongly than any one else the butcher and the legion of botchers who from the first days of lithography swarmed in a field where the heavens or the other place was the only boundary.

"These knew nothing of typecraft. They had no traditions except the German washtub, and of it they remembered nothing but the turbid suds. They were not bound by any limitations, and could run their degeneracies in a diagonal or double diagonal, circle, pyramid, oval, or triangle as they pleased. They could design their atrocities in the shape of a funerary urn or a memorial cross with ease, and the name of the deceased was beauty. The chaste and dignified black-letter and Old Face in their productions sprouted horns and were dishonoured, grew beards and senile, went crazed, corybantic, and vertiginous before dropping into G.P.I. They bellied out to obesity; they were eviscerated and herring-gutted; they developed macrocephaly and micropodism simultaneously, and for variety made them microcephaly and macropodism. Nor was any symmetry wanting. They suffered from goitre and elephantiasis, clubfoot and dropsy, lordosis and arthri-

tis. They achieved crassitude and macilency in the same line of letters; they reached latitudes and longitudes that no typefounder's chart had ever shown. The alphabets were coarctate and incrassated by turns, but nothing long. They thickened to Dorics, shrieked to hysterics, shrank to hairlines. If metamorphosis might be predicted of that which was crude amorphy they accomplished the change, as they did every negation of form and elegance, aesthetics and symmetry. They outhunned Attila in the ferocity of their vandalism.

"It would not have mattered quite so much if the original offences had been the only ones, but they were not. Whatever the degree of atonia or asthenia, decrepitude or debility, fragility or flaccidity, their fecundity was never in doubt. The butchers' knives committed every abortion but the one which would have been welcomed; they perpetrated every mutilation but sterility. The degenerates swelled and pulluiated, farrowed their litters and spawned their monstrous shoals until the world of Caslon and Baskerville, Jenson and Bodoni and Aldus, became the world of Caliban, the home of a bastard brood with the blood of beauty on its hands.

"All this was done in the name of lettering, yet it was as nothing to what the botchers did in the sacred name of ornament. Every tiniest blank space that their letters did not cover their bad scrolls and crotchets and quavers and distortions did. The simplest bit of work was sufficient excuse for an outbreak of blains and wems, blotches and wens, pimple and fungi, carbuncles and warts, and all manner of excrescences. And when they had done it all they reversed their designs, so that having inflicted them upon us in relief we had to endure them all over again in intaglio.

"Then came the crowning tragedy of all. The public liked it, asked for more of it, could not have enough of it. We should remember this and refrain from sneering at the craftsman. His grandfather in respect of the aesthetic standard was what our grandfathers made him. . . . No lettering became too vile for the typefounder to defile his moulds with; his ornaments were but a copy albeit an improved copy of the worst that the butchers carved. The insane contortions of typographical arrangement—the diagonal settings and diamonds of the compositor—were the abortions of the botchers translated to another sphere. With brass rule and shears the printer even tried to fashion landscapes and seascapes in type. In the great rout the eagles trailed the dust; the colophons of Berthelet and Day and Copland were engulfed in the mire."

Such is the description of conditions pre-

SOAP AND COSMETIC ADS PIONEER WITH FINER ADVERTISING ART

These reduced full page ads from St. Nicholas Magazine, 1886 to 1889, show a complete break with earlier tradition and the introduction of specially designed formats. The infant's bath is depicted with delicacy and tenderness; the perfume ads are early attempts at "atmosphere."

vailing during the last quarter of the Nineteenth Century, the period ushered in by the great Philadelphia Centennial Exposition in 1876. From all commercial aspects the Centennial was the most important single event of the times. It served as a healthful stimulus on all business and industrial progress, and had a particularly exciting effect upon the growth of advertising and the pictorial arts. The exhibits in the various buildings were crowded with displays of new products. Scattered throughout the halls were to be seen colorful handbills, cards, folders and announcements—the inevitable corollary representing a growing consciousness of sales promotion and advertising. It was the first time at a public gathering of vast millions that the audience was brought face to face with the force of advertising, not only by way of the many printed handouts but by the greatly increased volume of paid ads in the current periodicals. The numbers of newspapers and magazines multiplied at a phenomenal rate during this expansion period that marked the beginnings of electrical development. The mail-order business, starting its infancy during the seventies, forged ahead with very spirited activity. This necessitated printed catalogs, price lists, illustrated folders and supplements. The merchandise offered varied greatly, but one fact soon became an obvious axiom: pictures sold more goods. The wood engravers were pressed into service to supply this need, their illustrations becoming cold and factual in the interest of selling, yet serving to enliven the millions of mail-order catalogs that found their way into rural mail boxes all over the country. Cheaper postal rates helped obtain wider distribution, the penny postcard having become effective in 1873, followed by the two-cent letter rate ten years later.

It will be recalled that during the closing years of the Eighteenth and early in the Nineteenth Century there began to appear both copper and wood engraved trade cards in one color. During the seventies and eighties the form for these bits of curious advertising ephemera hit its highest peak, developing into a special phase of advertising art technique that blazed into glorious ascendency. Thousands upon thousands of quaint printed and lithographed cards made their appearance until the avalanche reached epidemic proportions. Designs ran the gamut of gay whimsicality to silly comic Valentines, from gaudy lithoed affairs to tinselled and die-cut varieties. Subjects included floral prints, animals, birds, landscapes, western and cowboy scenes, genre settings and "arty" compositions of all kinds. Often the advertiser's message and imprint appeared on the front or pictorial side, while more considerate merchants relegated their commercial sentiments to the reverse.

Whatever the reason, whether "collector's instinct" or not, the "card craze," as it became known, soon swept the country. The cards were avidly collected, traded and swapped. They found their way into special albums and a more permanent resting place alongside the family album on the parlor table. The absence of any colored pictures in quantities made these miniatures the more desirable and some were even framed and put up on living room walls. Recently, the *Saturday Evening Post*, in a feature story showing over a dozen of these in color, remarked:

"It was an age of wonders: bar soap, hay forks, mowing machines, lawn mowers—and all of them 'patent,' which seemed to suggest secrets of great value. Manufacturers were putting out bright pictures of these marvels, and the local dealer handed the cards to good customers with his compliments. Collecting them became, as they called it, a 'craze.' The cards were prized for two reasons. Colored pictures were rare. So were good heat, warm water, music, leisure and 'style.' The country was hungry for comforts and refinements. Undoubtedly, the cards speeded public acceptance of many new ideas. But they also performed the same service a movie of penthouse life does for the girl who lives in the third floor rear. The 'card craze' died in the 90's. Now the cards are once again collectors' items, as Americana."

THE PLATES

The illustrations shown on the following plates have been taken, for the most part, from type specimen books representative of the nineteenth century. A careful inspection of these volumes reveals that the cuts not only appear repeatedly in subsequent issues, but in the pages of several different foundries as well. A listing of these source books will be found in the Appendix, together with notes on the plates.

1

2

3

4

5

6

1

2

3

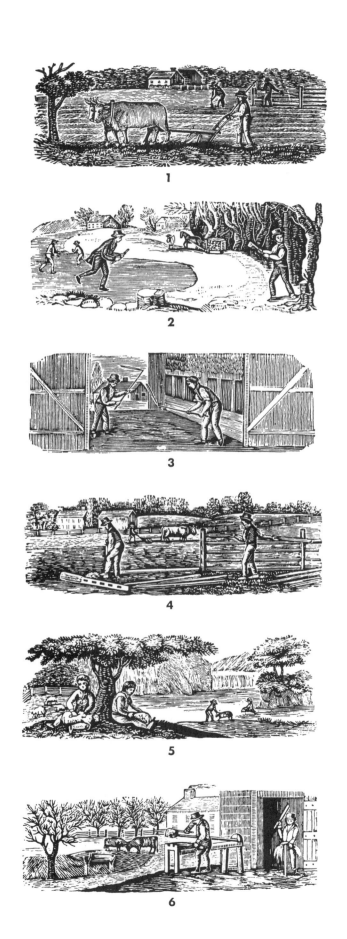

1

2

3

4

5

6

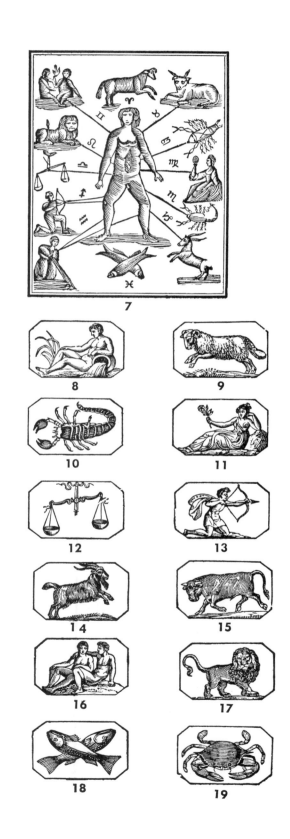

7

8

9

10

11

12

13

14

15

16

17

18

19

JANUARY

FEBRUARY

MARCH

APRIL

MAY

JUNE

JULY

AUGUST

SEPTEMBER

OCTOBER

NOVEMBER

DECEMBER

1

2

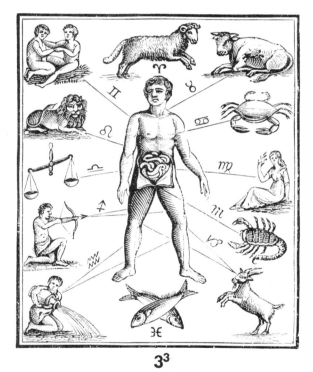

3³

4

5

1

2

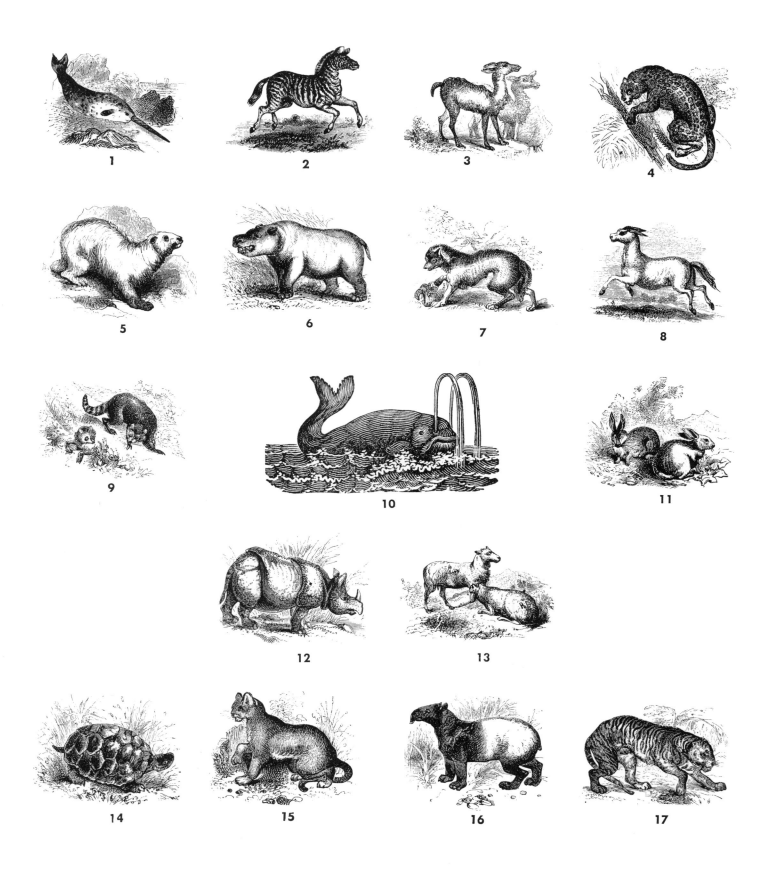

1

2

3

4

5

6

7

8

9

10

11

12

13

14

15

16

17

1

2

3

4

5

6

7

8

9

10

11

12

13

1

2

3

4

5

6

7

8

9

1

2

3

4

5

6

1

2

3

4

5

6

7

8

9

10

11

12

13

14

1

2

3

4

5

6

7

8

9

10

11

12

13

14

15

16

17

1

2

3

4

5

6

7

8

9

10

11

12

13

14

15

16

17

1

2

1

2

3

1

2

1

1911
Packard Eighteen
Landaulet

2

3

1

2

3

4

1

2

3

4

2

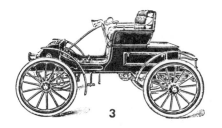

3

1

4

1

2

3

4

5

6

7

8

9

10

11

12

13

1

2

3

4

5

6

7

8

9

10

1

2

3

4

5

6

7

8

9

10

2

3

4

5

1

6

7

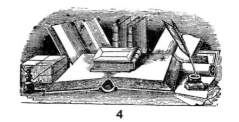

8

9

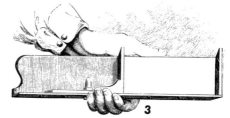

10

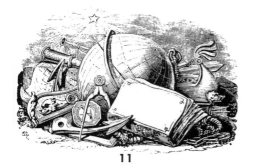

11

2

3

4

5

6

7

8

9

10

11

COMPACT
Book of Specimens
OF
Printing Types.

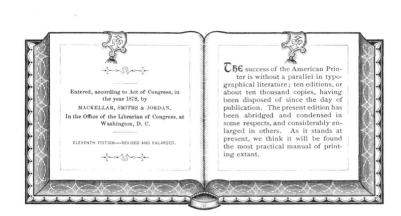

Entered, according to Act of Congress, in the year 1878, by
MACKELLAR, SMITHS & JORDAN,
In the Office of the Librarian of Congress, at Washington, D. C.

ELEVENTH EDITION—REVISED AND ENLARGED.

THE success of the American Printer is without a parallel in typographical literature; ten editions, or about ten thousand copies, having been disposed of since the day of publication. The present edition has been abridged and condensed in some respects, and considerably enlarged in others. As it stands at present, we think it will be found the most practical manual of printing extant.

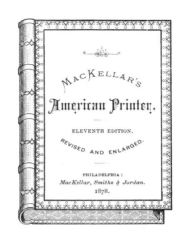

MACKELLAR'S
American Printer.

ELEVENTH EDITION.
REVISED AND ENLARGED.

PHILADELPHIA:
MacKellar, Smiths & Jordan.
1878.

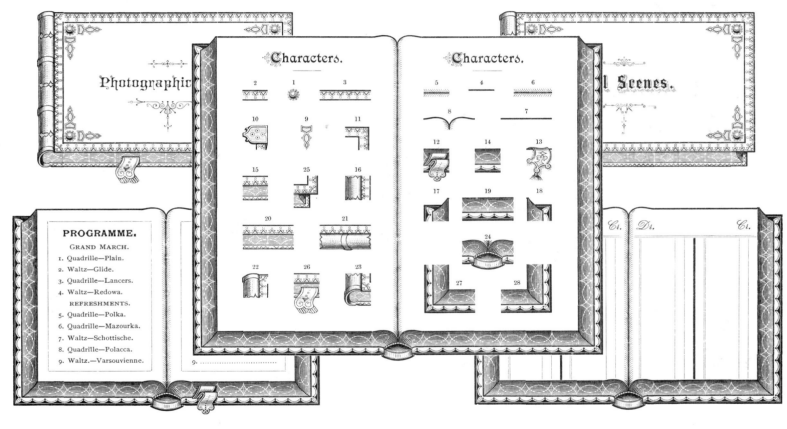

Photographic

Characters.

Characters.

l Scenes.

PROGRAMME.
GRAND MARCH.
1. Quadrille—Plain.
2. Waltz—Glide.
3. Quadrille—Lancers.
4. Waltz—Redowa.
REFRESHMENTS.
5. Quadrille—Polka.
6. Quadrille—Mazourka.
7. Waltz—Schottische.
8. Quadrille—Polacca.
9. Waltz.—Varsouvienne.

TYPE-FOUNDERS and others are respectfully notified that we reserve all rights in our new Cuts, bearing a copyright notice, and any infringement on the same will be legally contested.

ELEVENTH
BOOK OF SPECIMENS
MACKELLAR, SMITHS & JORDAN.

This new Border Series admirably fills a place hitherto unoccupied among the appliances of the Typographic Art. We present it to the craft as another evidence of our desire to place within their reach every means of diversifying the appearance of their skilful handiwork.

MacKellar, Smiths & Jordan.

1

2

3

4

5

6

7

8

1

2

3

4

5

6

7

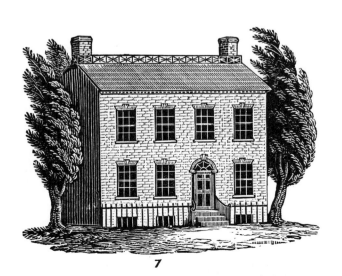

8

1

4

3

2

5

6

7

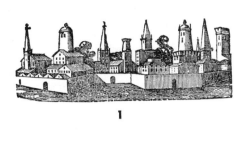

1

2

3

4

1

2

3

4

5

6

7

8

9

10

11

12

13

14

15

16

17

18

1

2

3

1

2

3

4

5

1

2

3

1

2

3

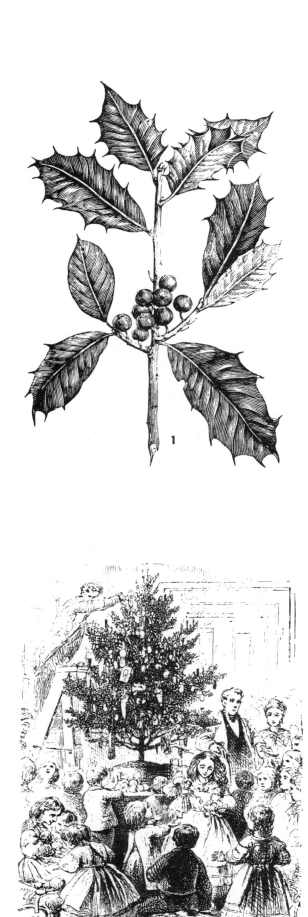

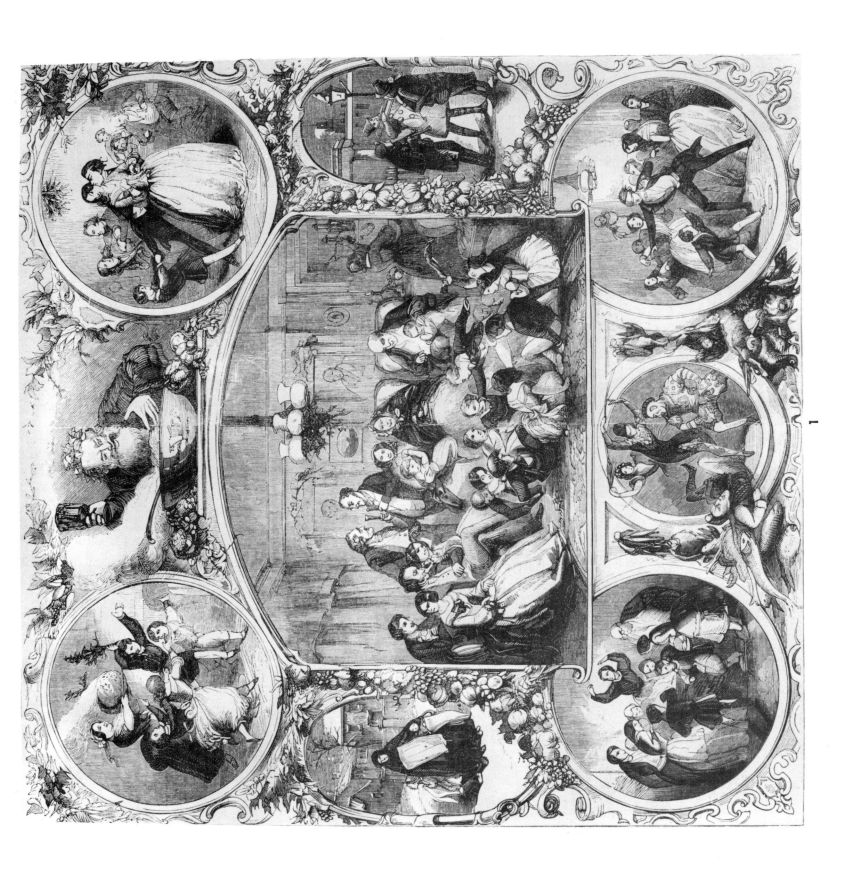

1

2

3

4

5

6

7

8

CRANDALL'S
LIVELY HORSEMAN.

MERRY CHRISTMAS

SANTA CLAUS.

1

2

3

4

5

6

7

8

1

2

3

4

5

6

7 8 9 10 11 12 13 14 15

16 17 18 19

20 21 23

1

2

3

4

5

6

1

2

3

4

5

6

7

LETTERS PATENT
E. CHESTERMAN,
NEW-YORK.

E PLURIBUS UNUM

8

UNITED STATES OF AMERICA
E PLURIBUS UNUM

9

E PLURIBUS UNUM

10

1

2

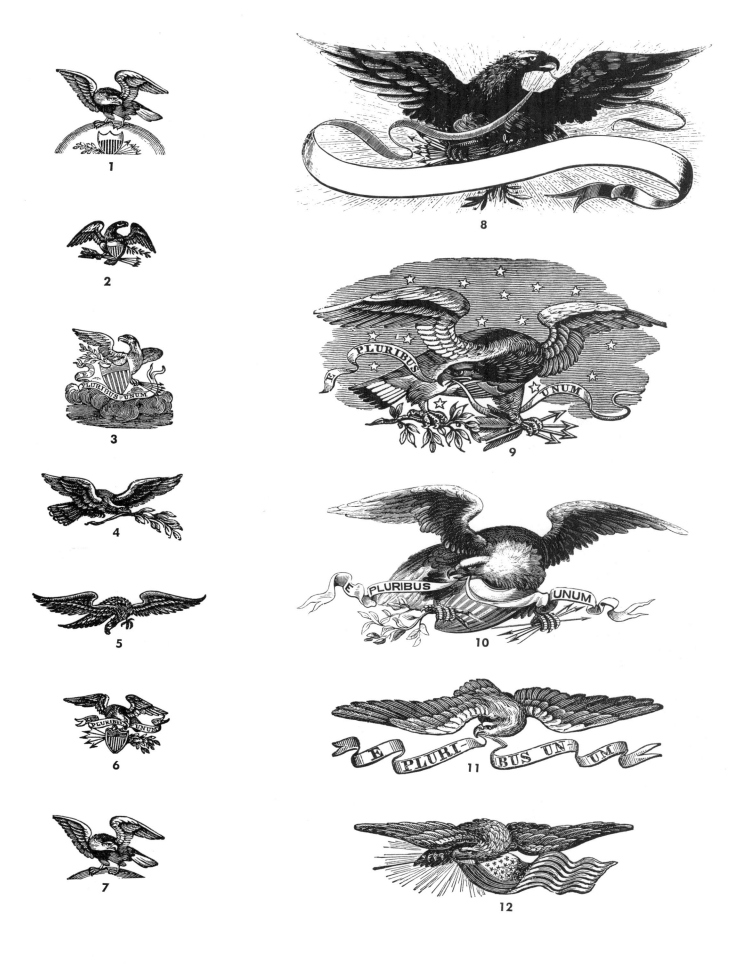

1

2

3

4

5

6

7

8

9

10

11

12

THE CONSTITUTION FOREVER.

THE UNION AND

L. JOHNSON & CO.

1

2

3

4

5

1

2

3

4

5

6

7

8

1

2

3

4

5

6

7

8

1

2

3

4

5

6

7

8

9

10

1

2

3

4

5   6

1

2

3

4

5

6

7

8

9

10

1

3

2

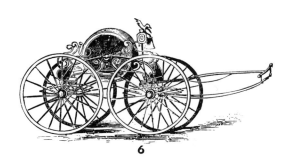

4

5

6

7

8

9

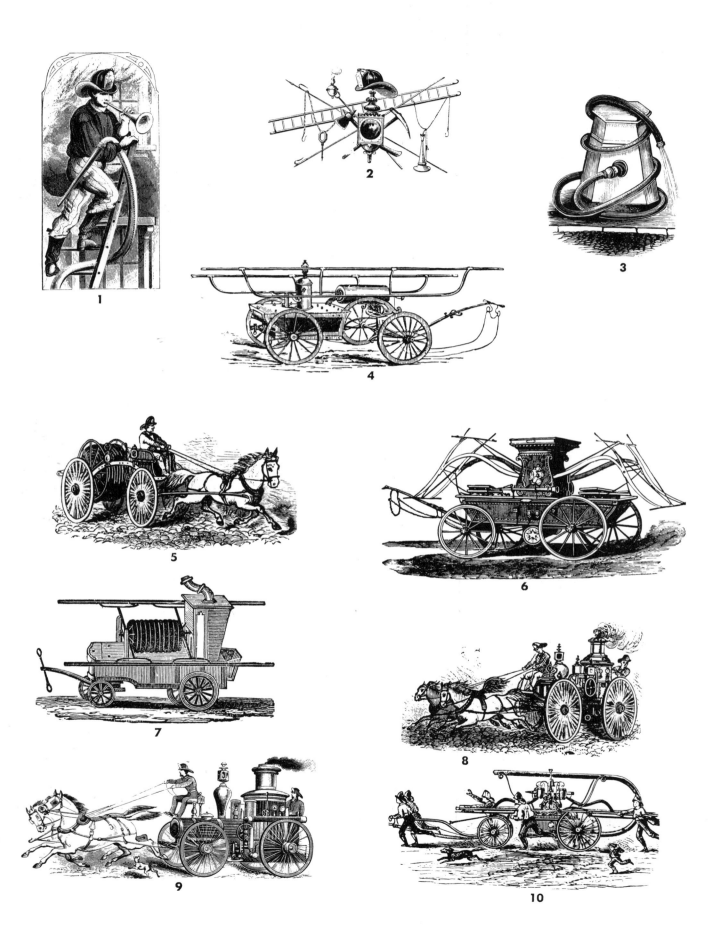

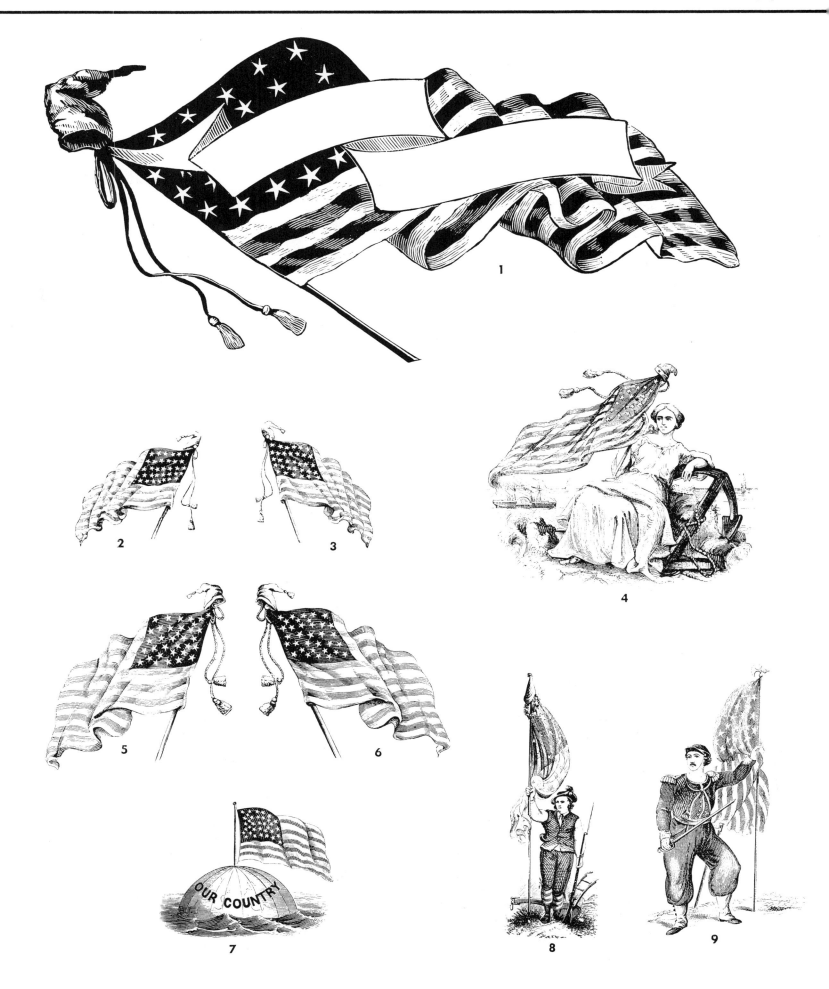

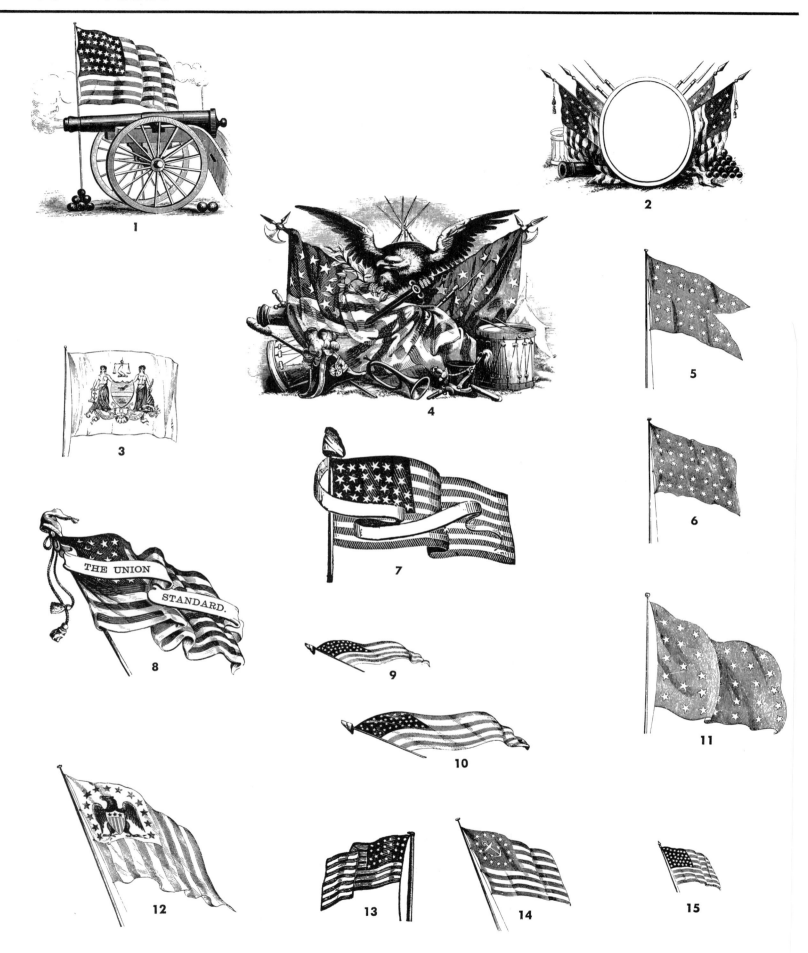

1

2

3

4

5

6

7

8

9

10

11

12

13

14

15

THE UNION

STANDARD.

1

2

3

4

5

6

7

8

9

10

11

12

13

14

15

16

17

18

19

20

1

2

3

4

5

6

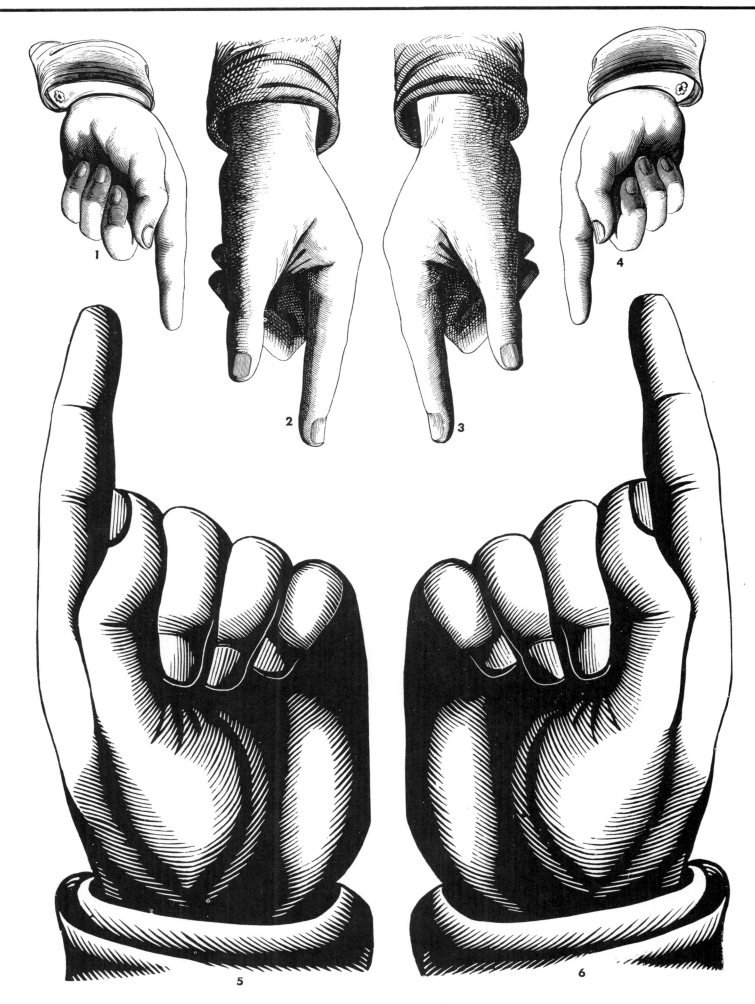

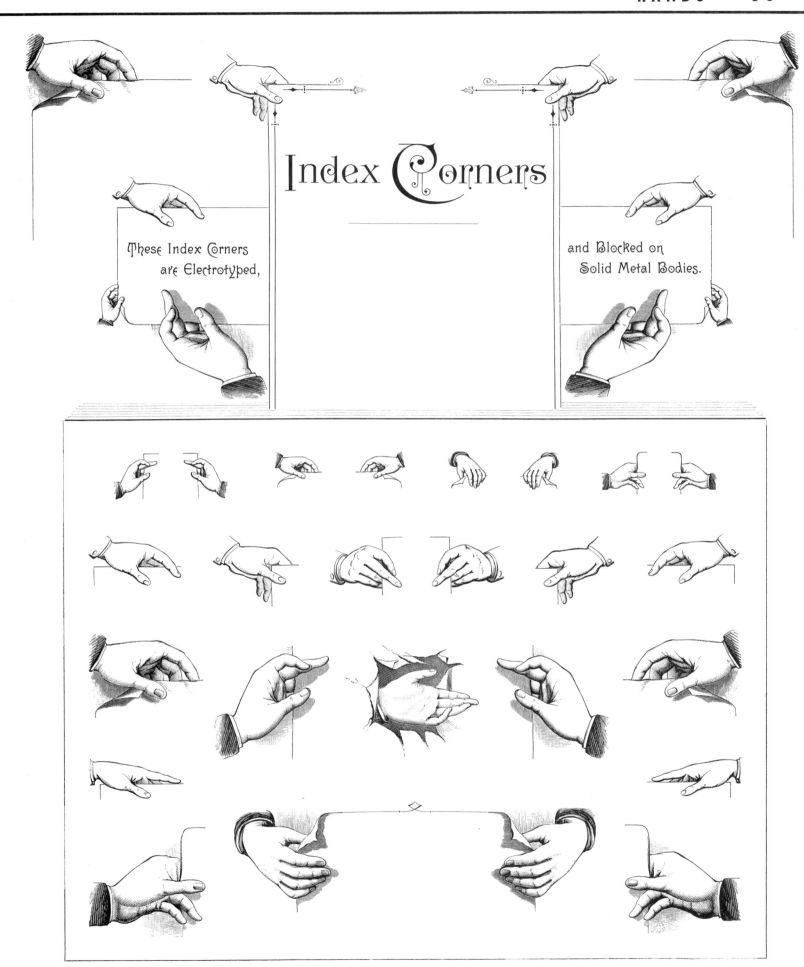

Index Corners

These Index Corners are Electrotyped,

and Blocked on Solid Metal Bodies.

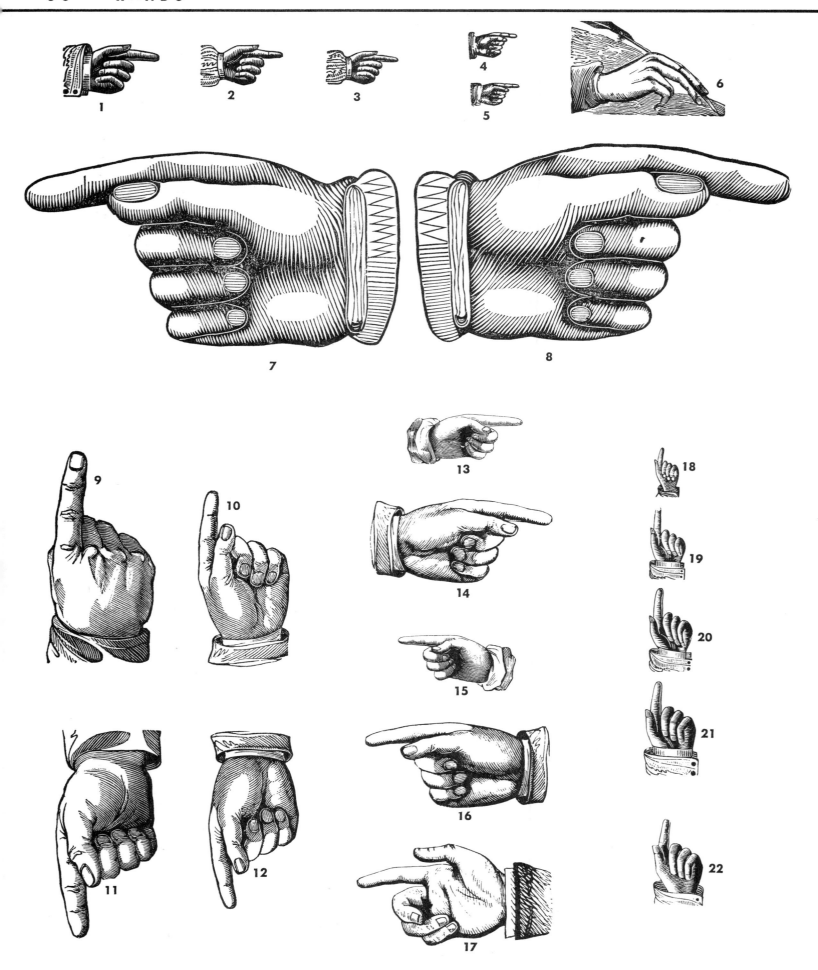

1

2

3

4

5

6

7

8

9

10

11

12

13

14

15

16

17

18

19

20

21

22

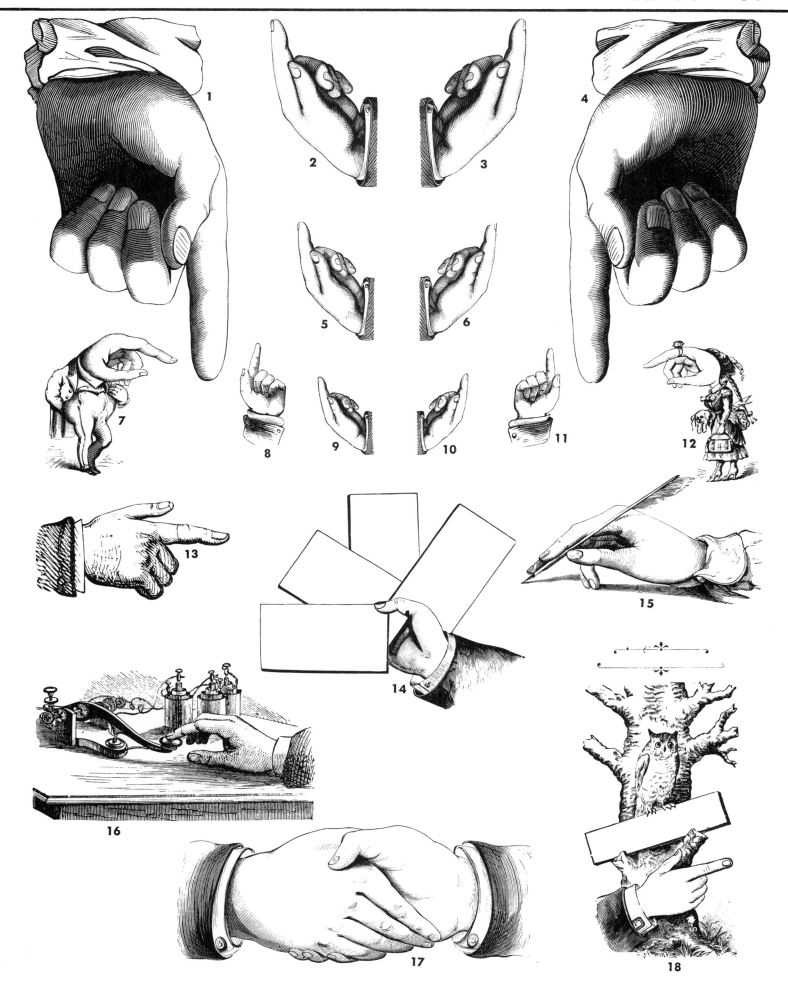

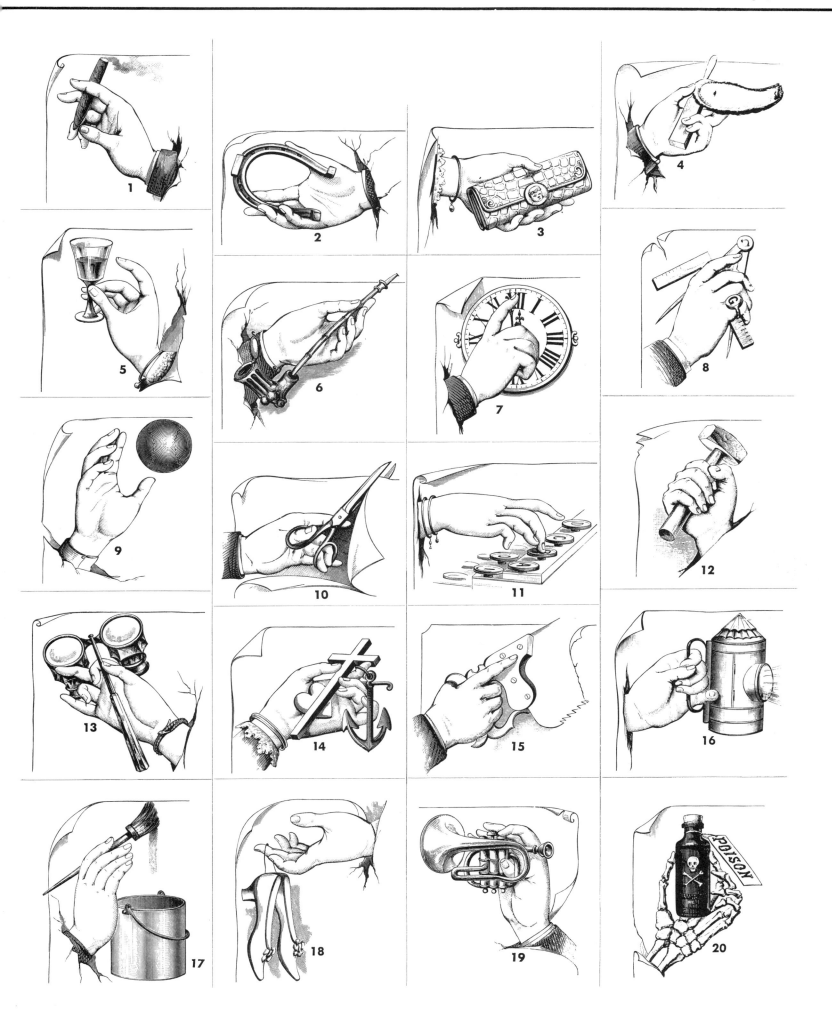

1

2

3

4

5

6

1

2

3

4

5

6

7

1

2

1

2

3

1

2

L. JOHNSON & CO.

1

1

2

1

2

3

4

5

1

2

3

4

5

1

2

3

1

2

3

4

5

6

7

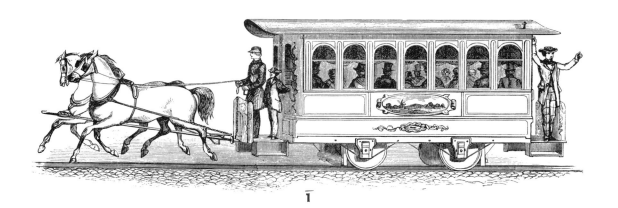

1

2

3

1

2

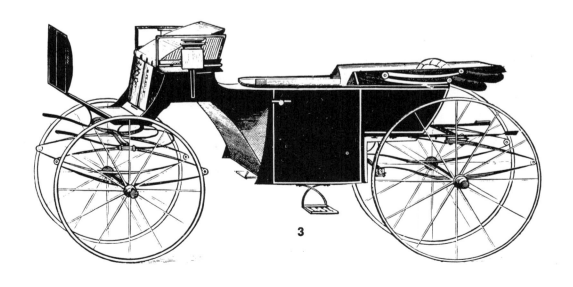

3

1

2

1

2

1

2

3

4

1

3

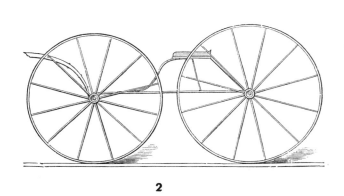

2

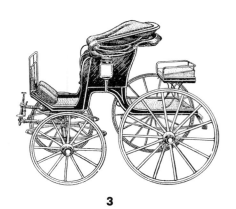

4

1

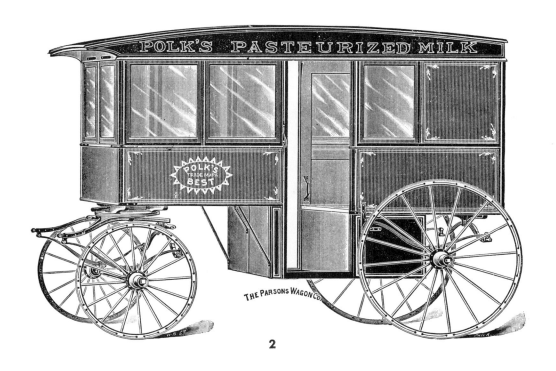

2

1

2

3

1

2

3

4

5

6

7

8

1

2

1

2

3

4

5

6

7

8

1

2

3

4

5

6

7

1

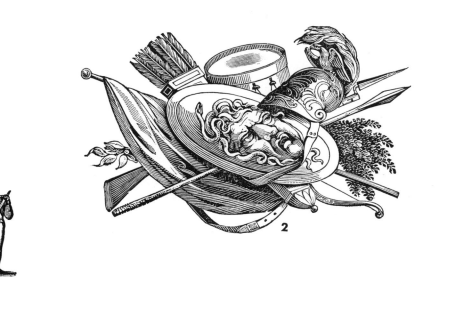

2

3

4

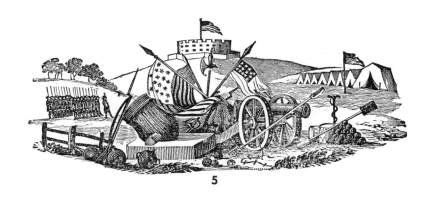

5

6

7

1

2

3

4

5

6

7

8

9

10

11

12

13

14

15

1

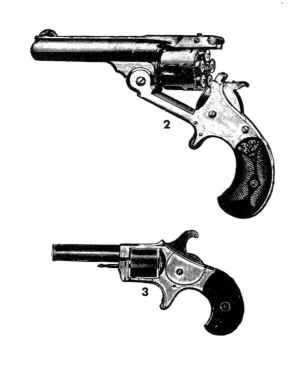

2

3

5

4

7

**SIMKINS,
CORDWAINER.**

FRENCH BOOTS
AND
CONGRESS GAITERS.

1

**PARLEZVOUS,
LADIES' SHOEMAKER**

PINCHEM STREET,
KIDVILLE.

2

**PLANEDEALER'S
HARDWARE STORE.**

Gimlets, Gouges, Tweezers, Pliers,
Pots and Kettles, Pans and Friers,
All Things for all Sorts of Buyers.

3

"Be off, you Scoundrel!
GO TO
CRISPIN'S BOOT STORE
IN PEG ALLEY,
And get a Pair for yourself for almost
Nothing! Officer,
let him go quick."

4

PHIDIAS ANGELO,
ARTIST IN
COATS, TROUSERS AND VESTS.

FITS WARRANTED
After Nature's Own Sweet Model.

5

**KARAT & DIAL,
CLOCK AND WATCHMAKERS.**

AGENTS FOR
Ladies' Year-Delaying Time-Keepers.

6

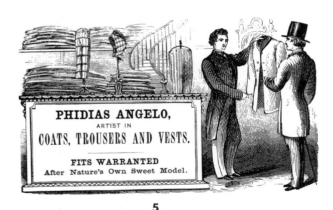

HOBBY-HORSES,
TOPS, SHUTTLECOCKS AND DOLLS,
Dancing Jacks,
DRUMS, TRUMPETS,
Bats and Balls.

7

SOLON CADDY'S
FINE
GROCERIES, WINES,
&c. &c.

8

1

2

3

4

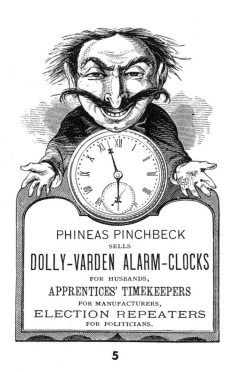

5

6

7

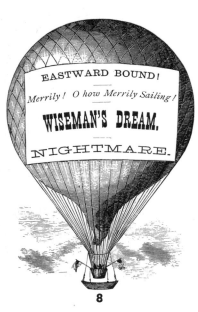

8

1

2

3

4

1

REFRESHMENT TICKET.

2

GREAT LAND ENTERPRISE AT LUNAVILLE!

ROUSING OPPORTUNITY!

Five Hundred Acres on the Sunny Side of the Moon to each Subscriber.

WITH LOTS OF ROCK FOR BUILDING PURPOSES!

When one half the stock is taken, an Atmospheric Engine will be erected in the crater of Popocatapetl to furnish refined air to the settlers, and a Steam Squirt will be placed on Goat Island to play water on the Moon, so that the inhabitants will have always enough—never too much, and never too little; thus avoiding the drouths and drenchings to which the earth's people are liable. Balloons also will be provided to start daily from different available points on the earth.

NOW IS THE TIME TO SUBSCRIBE!

5

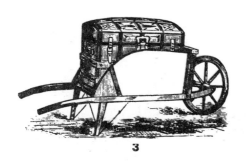

3

GET ALONG, JOSEY!

CHEAP FOR CASH.

4

LOOKOUT'S
REMEDY FOR
DISTURBERS OF THE PEACE,
NIGHT RINGS,
AND
INCORRIGIBLE BILLSTICKERS.

PROMPT! PENETRATING! PHYSICAL!

STICK NO BILLS

1

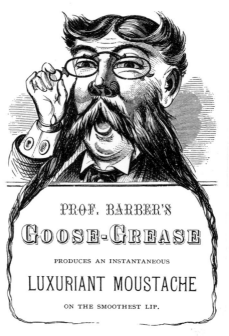

PROF. BARBER'S
GOOSE-GREASE
PRODUCES AN INSTANTANEOUS
LUXURIANT MOUSTACHE
ON THE SMOOTHEST LIP.

2

VOICE OF THE PEOPLE
IN FAVOUR OF THE
UNIVERSAL FLY-TRAP
NO SHUT-MOUTH GAME.

3

CRACK
PRIZE BOXES,
SURE TO CONTAIN
SOMETHING OF INTEREST
FOR ALL.

With Directions for getting out of a Tight Place.

4

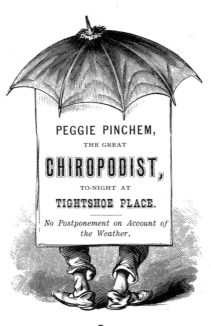

PEGGIE PINCHEM,
THE GREAT
CHIROPODIST,
TO-NIGHT AT
TIGHTSHOE PLACE.

No Postponement on Account of the Weather.

5

SAMUEL UPHEGOES
GIVES ATTENTION TO
Hoisting and Lowering
THINGS GENERALLY.

N.B.—No Connection with the Stock Market.

6

1

2

1

2

3

4

5

6

7

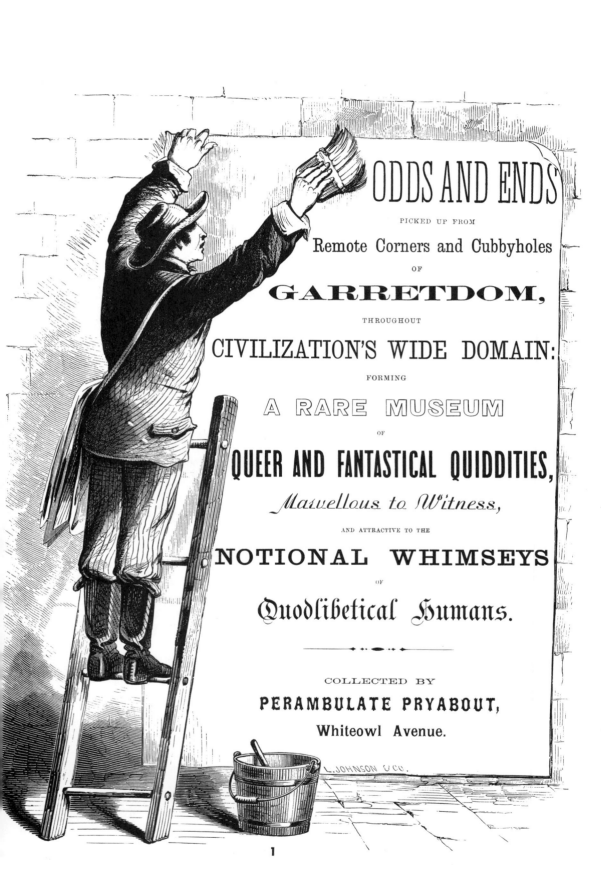

ODDS AND ENDS

PICKED UP FROM

Remote Corners and Cubbyholes

OF

GARRETDOM,

THROUGHOUT

CIVILIZATION'S WIDE DOMAIN:

FORMING

A RARE MUSEUM

OF

QUEER AND FANTASTICAL QUIDDITIES,

Marvellous to Witness,

AND ATTRACTIVE TO THE

NOTIONAL WHIMSEYS

OF

Quodlibetical Humans.

COLLECTED BY

PERAMBULATE PRYABOUT,

Whiteowl Avenue.

1

CAMERA & SUN,
Photographic Artists.
240 Attic Row,
PICTUREVILLE.

2

TAKE PARTICULAR NOTICE.

3

Notice to Travellers.

FURNITURE
REMOVED
During the Owner's Absence.

Proceeds Equally Divided by

Masculine Kleptomaniacs.

4

Little Fuss-and-Feathers
Pipes his morning song,
And chirpeth, chirpeth merrily
All the Summer long;
Chick, chick, chee!
O, come and see
What a right merrie
Birdie I be.

1

EXCELSIOR!

THE
DIGNITY
OF
LABOUR.

2

WALK UP, POOR FOLK!

~~100,000~~

EASY AND NOVEL WAYS

TO

MAKE MONEY.

Sure Guarantees, Ten Cents Each.

3

IMMENSE
ATTRACTION!
Two-Legged
DONKEY
ON
EXHIBITION.
AT
GAGTOWN.

TEMPLE OF FORTUNE
IN
SHINBONE ALLEY.
SHYLOCK,
POLICY VENDOR
Riches for the Million.

EXTRA!
News from
SEAT OF WAR!
CACKLETON
TAKEN!
**FOUL
SLAUGHTER!**
Rooster Defeated!

4

1

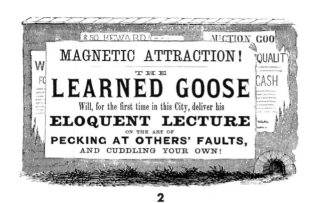

2

3

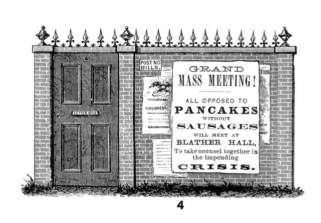

4

5

6

THE AMERICAN PRINTER.
Price, $1.50: by mail, $1.70.
MacKellar, Smiths & Jordan.

ESSAY ON PUNCTUATION.
Price, $1.50: by mail, $1.70.
MacKellar, Smiths & Jordan.

1

HORN, BUTCHER, DROVERS' MARKET, Stall 216.

2

LADIES' WEAR, DRESS GOODS, SHAWLS, Fine Silks, Laces, &c.
GIMCRACKE, IMPORTER DIRECT FROM PARIS.

3

Typographic Advertiser
Vol. XV. JANUARY, 1870. No. 1.
EDITED AND PUBLISHED BY
MacKellar, Smiths & Jordan,
NO. 606-614 SANSOM ST.,
PHILADELPHIA.
TYPE AND STEREOTYPE FOUNDING, ELECTROTYPING, WOOD ENGRAVING, &c. &c.

4

NOTICE! MEN, WOMEN, AND CHILDREN Are required to Appear AT THE STORE OF PETER CLEVER, ALL-SORTS ROW, And invest to the extent of their CASH! A VERMILION EDICT!

5

TOMTIT, DEALER IN WIND INSTRUMENTS, HAUTBOYS, WEATHERCOCKS, JEWSHARPS, AND PENNY WHISTLES.

6

HAVANA BALM, Virginia Cherry Sweet, GRANDMA'S NOSEGAY, YARA LIP-HONEY, AND OTHER DELICATE WEED CONCOCTIONS, JACOB NICOTIN, SMOKEVILLE.

7

"Love blows the Trumpet of Fame!" THAT'S SO! AND THUS THE BLAST! HIGHEST PRICES FOR OLD IRON, PEWTER, Lead, COPPER, ROPES AND RAGS, BY GUNNYBAGS.

8

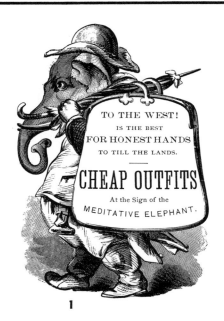

TO THE WEST!
IS THE BEST
FOR HONEST HANDS
TO TILL THE LANDS.

CHEAP OUTFITS
At the Sign of the
MEDITATIVE ELEPHANT.

1

All the Fair,
With Beaming Eye and Curly Hair,
SING IN PRAISE OF THE
ACME
HAIR DYE.

*It will curl straight hair, and
straighten curled hair.*

2

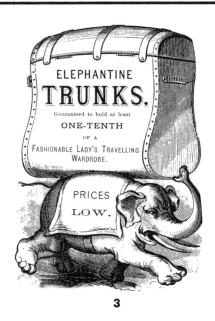

ELEPHANTINE
TRUNKS,
Guaranteed to hold at least
ONE-TENTH
OF A
FASHIONABLE LADY'S TRAVELLING
WARDROBE.

PRICES
LOW.

3

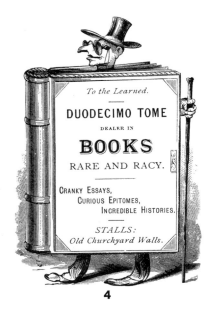

To the Learned.
DUODECIMO TOME
DEALER IN
BOOKS
RARE AND RACY.

CRANKY ESSAYS,
CURIOUS EPITOMES,
INCREDIBLE HISTORIES.

*STALLS:
Old Churchyard Walls.*

4

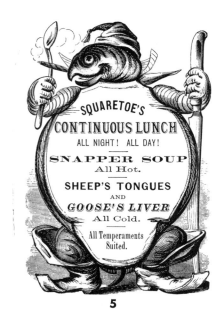

SQUARETOE'S
CONTINUOUS LUNCH
ALL NIGHT! ALL DAY!
SNAPPER SOUP
All Hot.
SHEEP'S TONGUES
AND
GOOSE'S LIVER
All Cold.
All Temperaments
Suited.

5

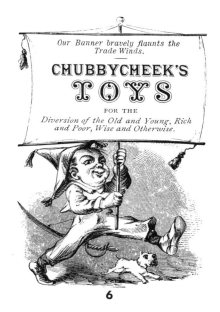

*Our Banner bravely flaunts the
Trade Winds.*
**CHUBBYCHEEK'S
TOYS**
FOR THE
*Diversion of the Old and Young, Rich
and Poor, Wise and Otherwise.*

6

*They sing it in the parlours,
It is whistled all about,
They play it on hand-organs,
THAT*
**STUBB'S
BLACKING**
IS THE
BEST SHINER OUT.

Only 10 Cents a Box.

7

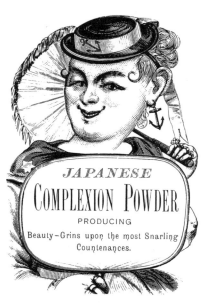

JAPANESE
COMPLEXION POWDER
PRODUCING
Beauty-Grins upon the most Snarling
Countenances.

8

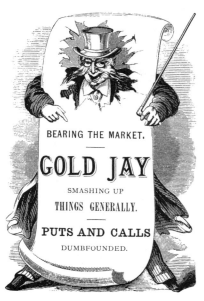

BEARING THE MARKET.
GOLD JAY
SMASHING UP
THINGS GENERALLY.
PUTS AND CALLS
DUMBFOUNDED.

9

1

2

3

4

5

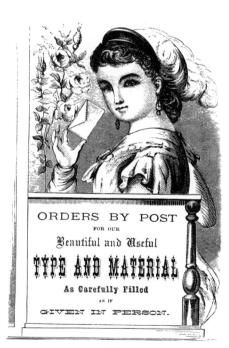

6

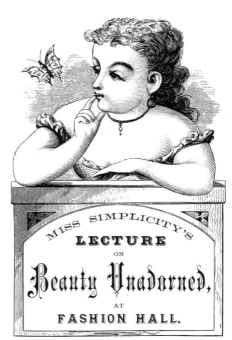

MISS SIMPLICITY'S
LECTURE
ON
Beauty Unadorned,
AT
FASHION HALL.

2

REFLECTIONS
ON THE
Morality of Founders
WHO CRIB
OUR ORIGINAL CUTS.

1

ROAD TO HEALTH.
Up in the Morning Early.
HERE SHE GOES, THERE SHE GOES.

3

EVERLASTING LOVE-KNOTS
SECURELY TIED BY
PARSON SILVERTONGUE,
CATHEDRAL PORCH,
BLUEBEARDTOWN.

4

TILE & CASTOR, FASHIONABLE HATTERS.

FURS, MISSES' BONNETS, GENTLEMEN'S HEAD-PIECES, &c. &c.

1

MRS. BONNETLOVE, MILLINER.

PARISIAN STYLE: AMERICAN TASTE: EXQUISITE CONTOUR.

2

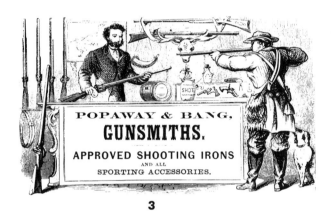

POPAWAY & BANG, GUNSMITHS.

APPROVED SHOOTING IRONS AND ALL **SPORTING ACCESSORIES.**

3

SCHNIPP'S **ARTISTIC TONSORIAL SALOON**

HAIR CUT PHYSIOLOGICALLY.

Leeching, Cupping, and Bleeding.

4

MORTAR BLUEPILL, Graduate of the College of Pharmacy. *Practical Pharmaceutist.*

PRESCRIPTIONS CAREFULLY COMPOUNDED.

5

PUMPKINVILLE STORE!

FRESH GOODS FROM THE EAST!

GEWGAWS FOR GIRLS! **TOMFOOLERIES FOR BOYS!** **FANCIES FOR WOMEN!** **Substantials for Men!**

TZADDI SHARPEYE, MAIN STREET.

6

SUNBEAM, **PHOTOGRAPHER,** 123 Skyhigh Building, HELIOTROPOLIS.

Likenesses twice as natural as Life.

7

T. POTT, DEALER IN **AMBROSIAL TEAS,** SWEETMEATS, **EDIBLE BIRDSNESTS,** &c. &c.

8

JACOB FAIRDEALER
SELLS
TEA AND COFFEE,
WHEN DUTY FREE,
AT A REDUCTION—NOT AN INCREASE.

Anti-Tea-and-Coffee-Corner Man.

1

HATCHET & GIMLET'S
FASHIONABLE
HARDWARE STORE.

Gold Coffee Pots. | Silver Skittels.
Parlour Cooking Stoves.

2

FELT & PLUSH,
CHARACTERISTIC HATTERS,
AND DEALERS IN
PERSUASIVE ROCKY MOUNTAIN BEAVERS,
NOBBY CASTORS,
Indian Skull Caps, &c.

3

DEMIJOHN'S
CHOICE
LIQUORS.

Drawn from the Wood.

4

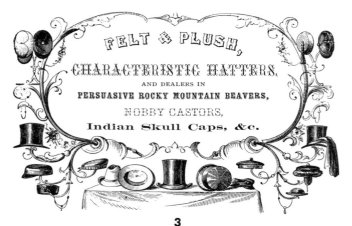

BREVES & SEMIBREVES,
JOBBERS IN
Dulcet Symphonies,
JEWS-HARPS AND BASS DRUMS.

Reference:—BOSTON JUBILEE.

5

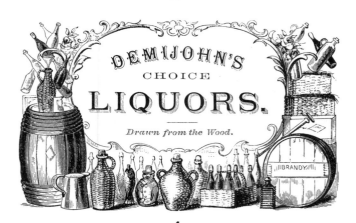

BULLOCK & CLEAVER,
DEALERS IN
NUTRITIOUS MEATS,
DAINTY GAME,
SAVORY PISCATORIAL TIDBITS.
CHOICE CUTS FOR ALL.

6

SNEEZER'S
INCOMPARABLE
ODOROUS SNUFFS,
SEGARS,
DELICIOUS FINE CUTS, ETC.

One Price for all Sexes and Colours.

7

MORTAR BLUEPILL,
Graduate of the College of Pharmacy,
PRACTICAL PHARMACEUTIST.

PRESCRIPTIONS CAREFULLY COMPOUNDED.

8

Universal Intelligencer.

Vol. XXIV.   APRIL, 1871.   No. 13.

HIGHLY INTERESTING!

LOVERS OF GENTLE CONSORTS,

Wives and Children,

Rightminded Brothers, Devoted Sisters,

FOND GRANDPAPAS,

Child-Spoiling Grandmammas,

MAIDEN AUNTIES,

GENEROUS UNCLES,

EXPECTANT NIECES,

AND

HAIRBRAINED NEPHEWS,

ALL,

Without Distinction of Age or Sex,

WILL FIND

KEENER'S CORN-SALVE

UNRIVALLED!

L. JOHNSON & CO.

1

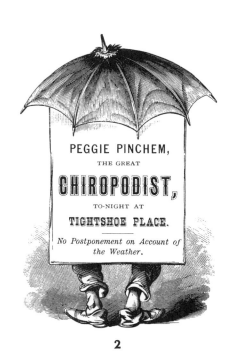

PEGGIE PINCHEM,

THE GREAT

CHIROPODIST,

TO-NIGHT AT

TIGHTSHOE PLACE.

No Postponement on Account of
the Weather.

2

All-Hallow-Eve.

NOCTURNAL RANGERS,

TAKE

WARNING!

No Signs to be Misplaced
Hereafter.

Growler Watchem.

3

FLORAL EXHIBITION.

4

Squatter Sovereignty.

Priority of Claim

NO, YOU DON'T, PUSSY!

The Old Bone of Contention.

5

1

2

3

5

4

6

7

8

9

10

1

2

3

4

5

6

7

8

9

10

11

1

2

3

4

5

6

1

2

3

4

5

Let her bang, ye Heroes!   Victory is Ours!

6

1

2

3

4

5

6

7

1

2

3

4

1

2

3

4

5

6

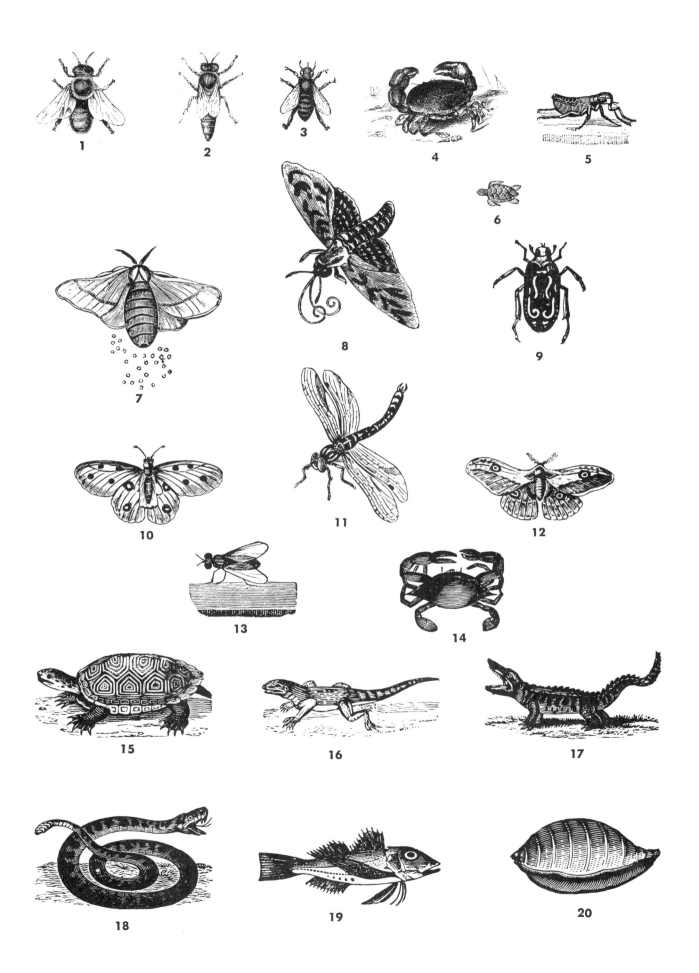

1

2

3

4

5

6

7

8

9

10

11

12

13

14

15

16

17

18

19

20

1

2

3

4

5

6

7

8

9

10

11

12

13

14

15

16

17

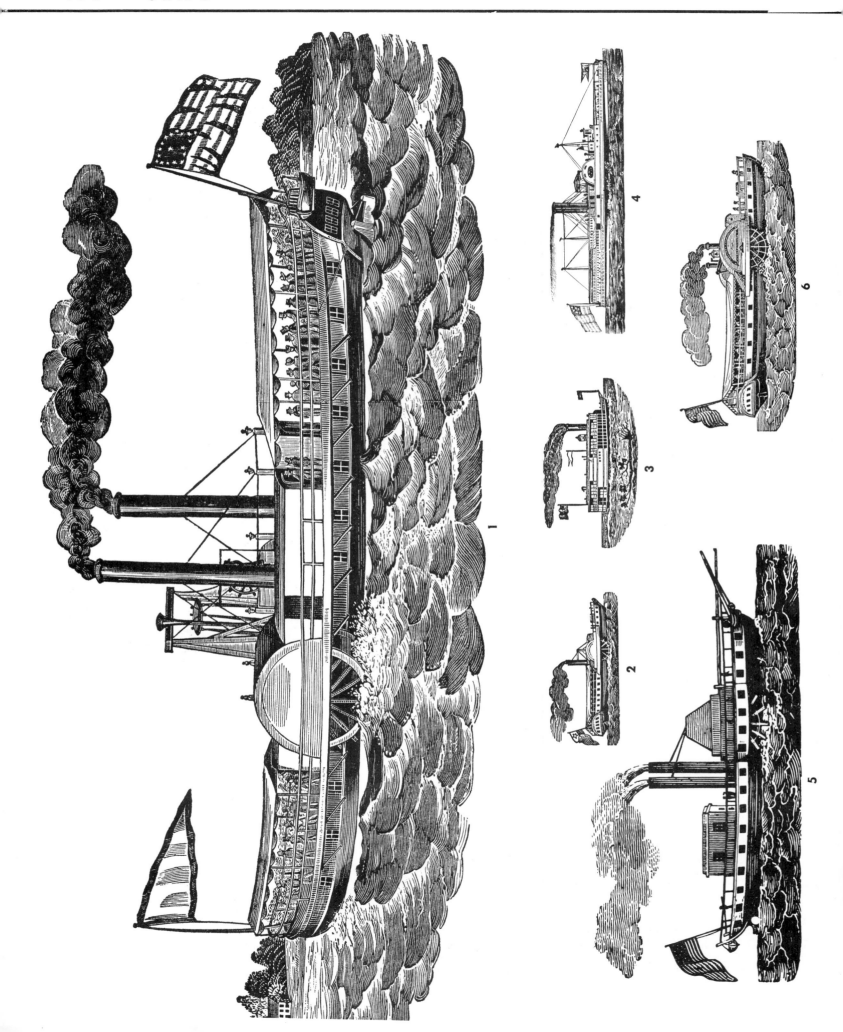

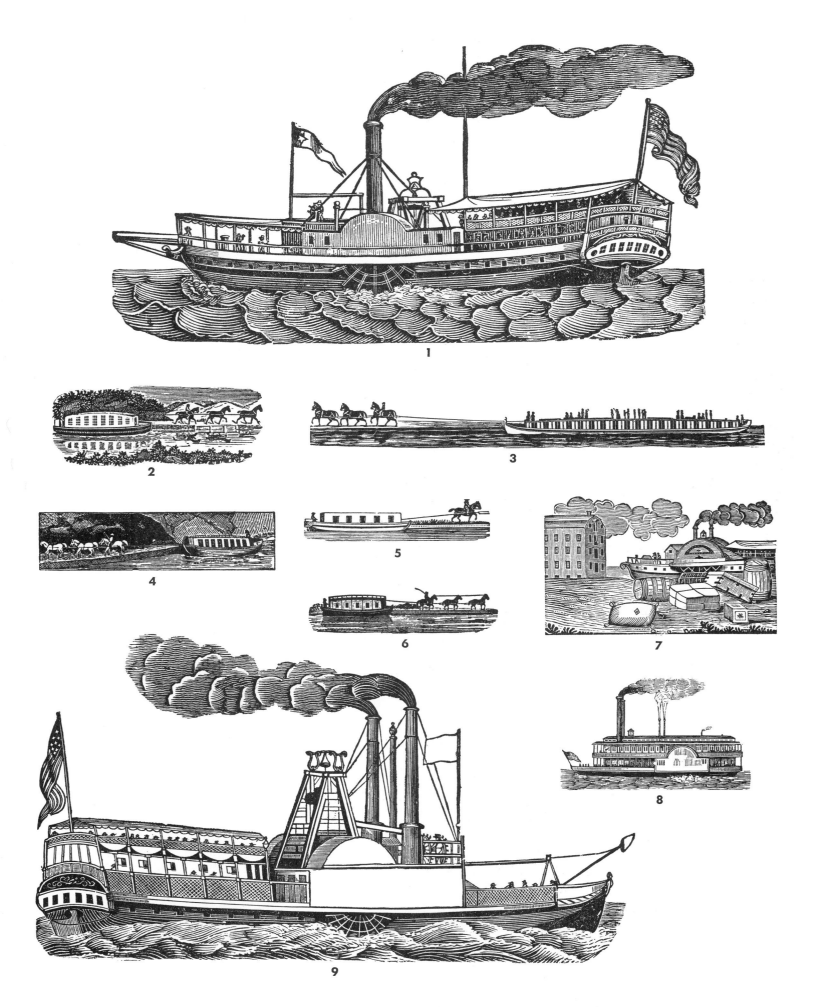

1

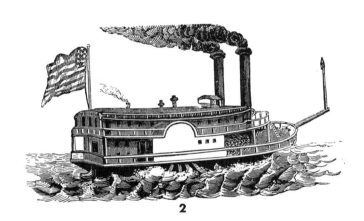

2

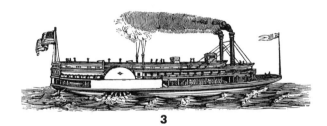

3

4

5

6

7

8

9

10

11

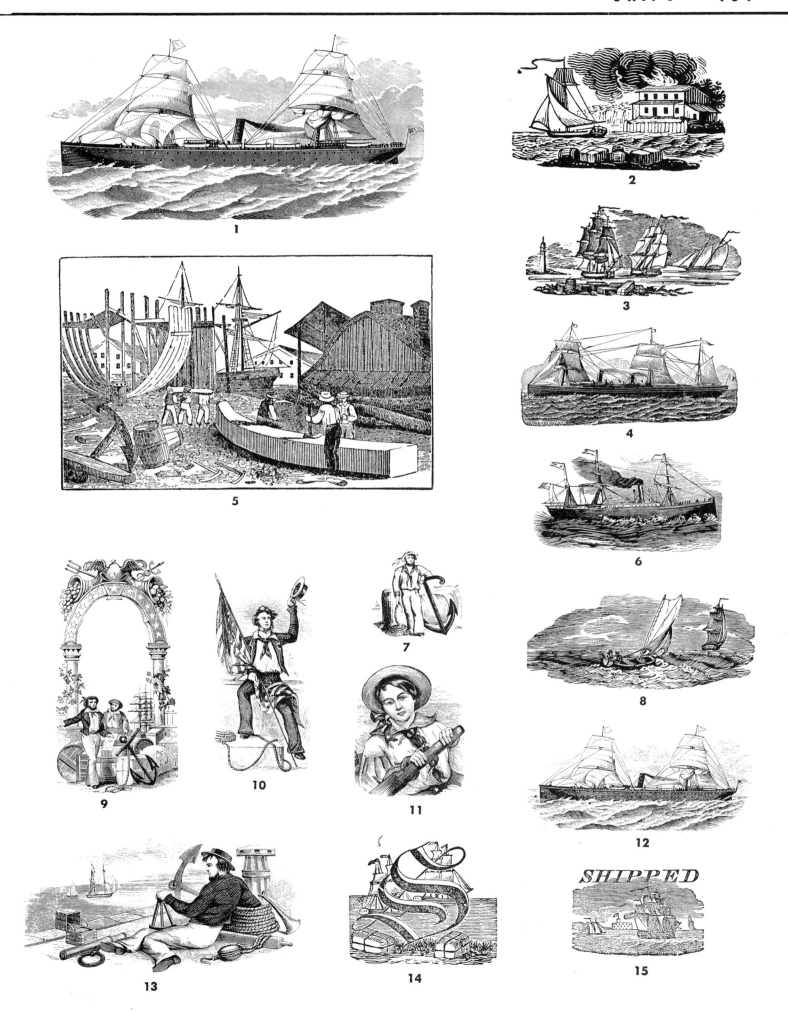

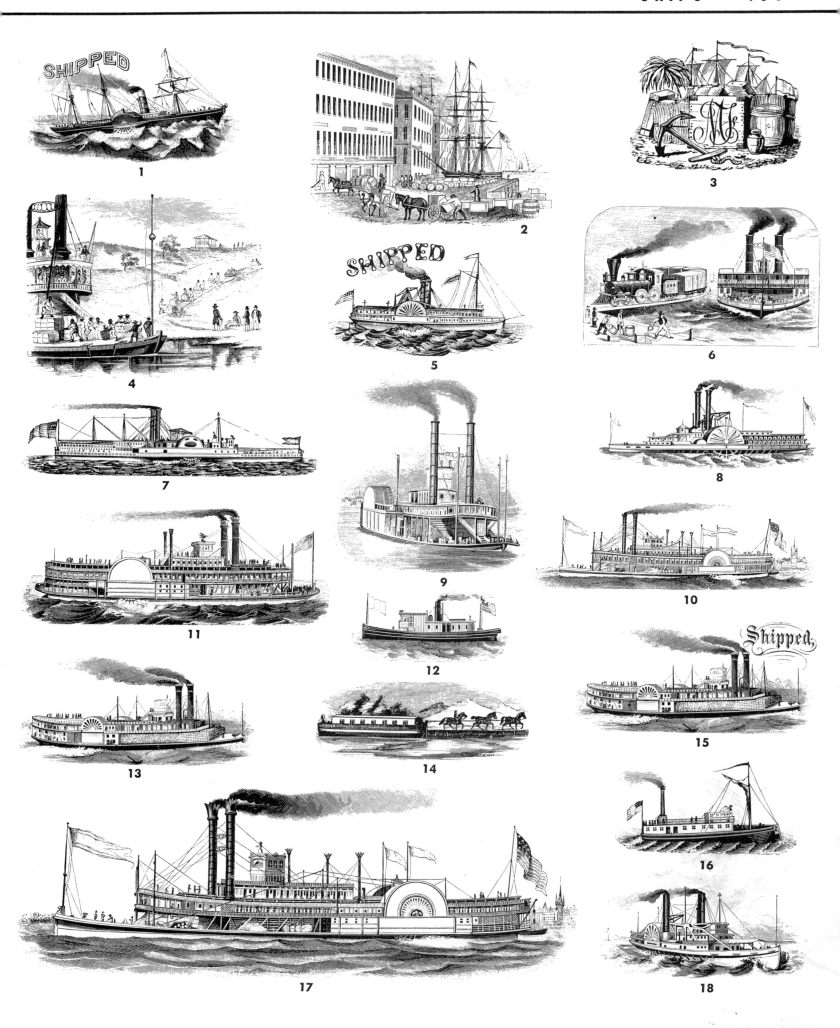

1

2

3

4

5

6

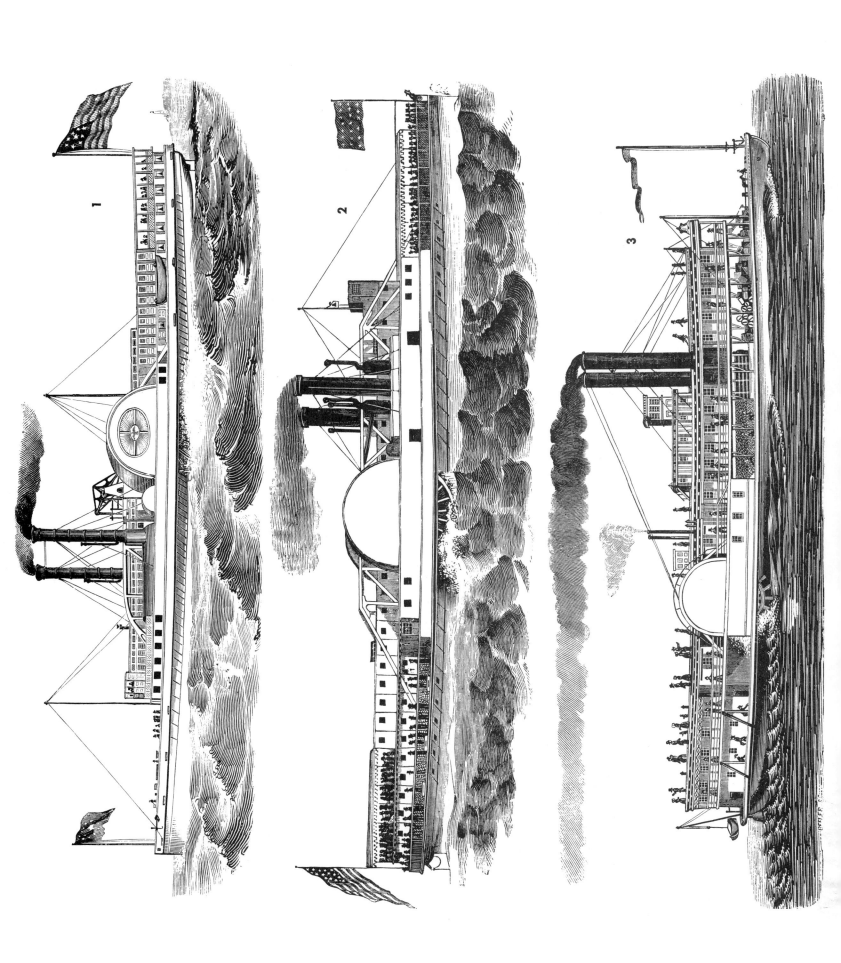

1

2

3

4

5

6

7

8

9

1

2

3

4

5

6

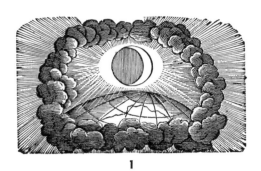

1

3

5

2

4

7

1

6

3

4

2

5

1

2

3

4

5

6

7

8

3

2

5

4

1

6

1

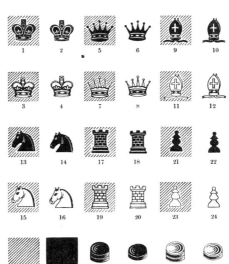

2

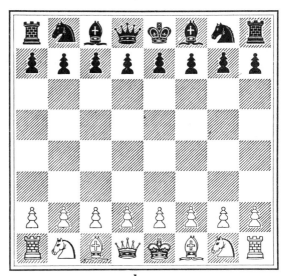

3

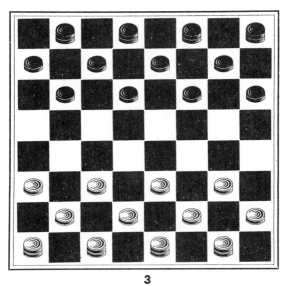

4

5

6

7

8

9

10

1

2

3

4   5

6

7

8

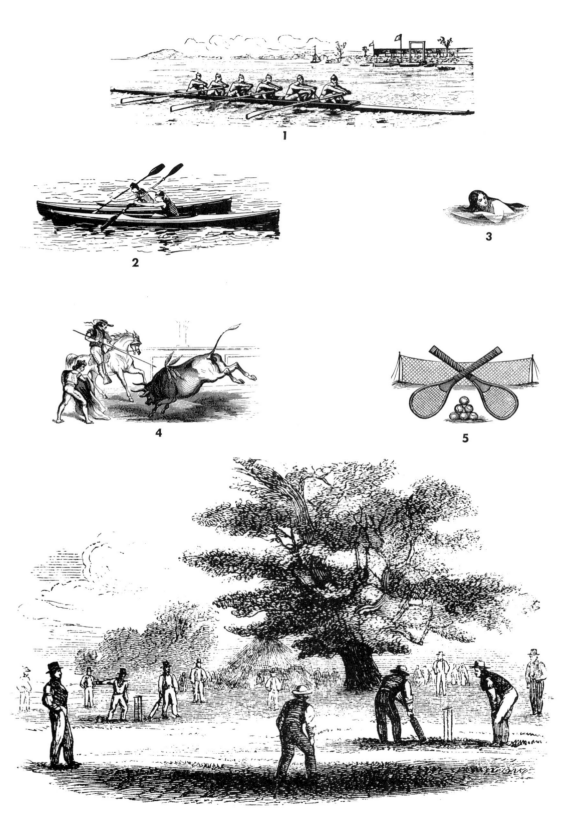

1

2

3

4

5

6

1

2

3

4

5

6

1

2

3

4

5

6

1

2

3

4

5

6

7

8

9

10

11

2

1

3

4

5

6

7

8

9

10

1

2

3

4

5

6

7

8

9

1

2

3

4

5

6

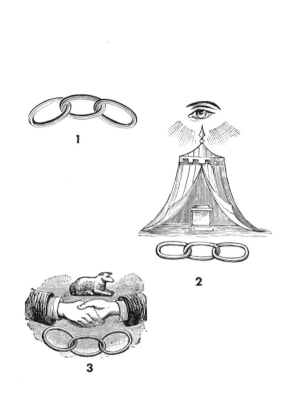

1

2

3

4

7

5

8

6

9

1

2

3

4

5

6

7

8

1

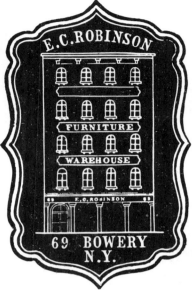

4

2

3

5

6

7

8

9

MILLINER.

MUSIC-DEALER.

NOTION-DEALER.

FURRIER.

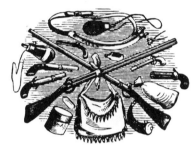

GUNSMITH.

HATTER.

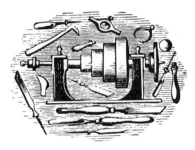

TURNER.

OPTICIAN.

FISHING-TACKLE.

TOBACCONIST.

TOY-DEALER.

TRUNK-MAKER.

BAKER.

WHEELWRIGHT.

WIRE-WORKER.

MINER.

CROCKERY.

TOBACCONIST.

HATTER.

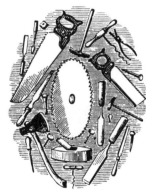

HARDWARE.

VICTUALLER.

DRUGGIST.

FARMER.

FLOUR-DEALER.

TAILOR.

TALLOW-CHANDLER.

TEA-DEALER.

STATIONER.

STEAM-ENGINE.

STOVE-MAKER.

PEN-DEALER.

PICKLES AND PRESERVES.

SADDLER.

SHIP-BUILDER.

SHIP-CHANDLER.

SHOE-FINDER.

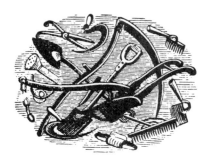

AGRICULTURAL IMPLEMENTS.

APOTHECARY.

ARTIFICIAL FLOWERS.

BASKET-MAKER.

BELL-HANGER.

BLACKSMITH.

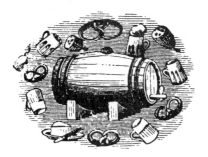

BREWER.

BRICKLAYER.

BRUSH-MAKER.

CARPENTER.

CARRIAGE-BUILDER.

CEDAR-COOPER.

1

2

3

4

5

6

1

2

3

4

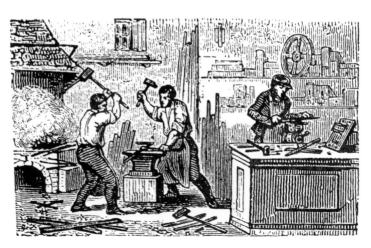

5

6

1

2

3

4

5

6

1

2

3

Wait

1

2

3

4

5

6

1

2

4

3

5

6

1 2 3
4 5 6
7 8 9
10 11 12
13 14 15

1

2

3

4

5

6

7

8

9

10

11

12

13

14

15

16

17

18
Prescriptions Carefully Compounded.

19
CHINA GLASS AND QUEENS WARE

20

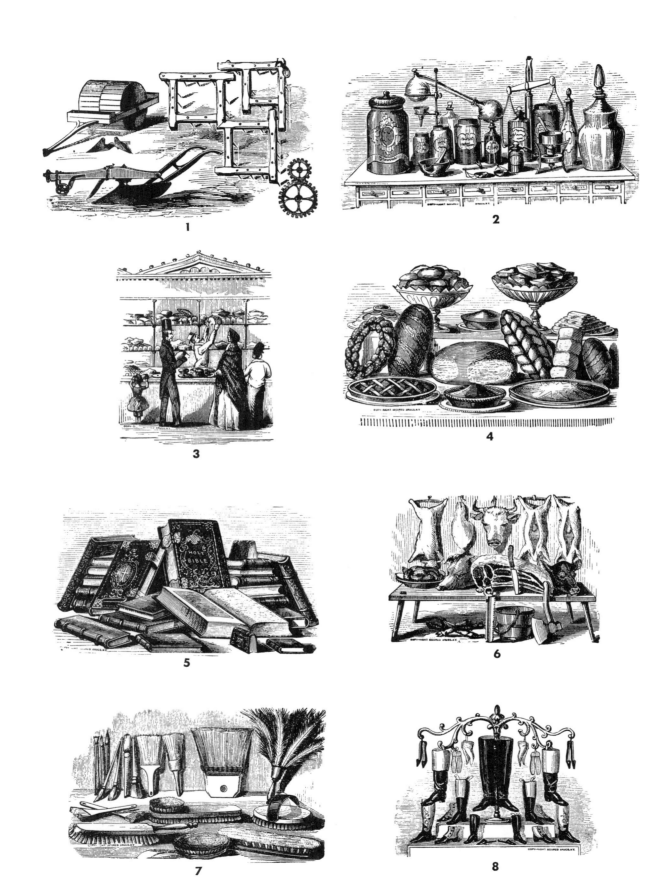

GEORGE J. HENKELS,

CITY CABINET   WAREROOMS,

173 Chestnut St Philadelphia.

Devereux Del.

1

GEORGE J. HENKELS.
CITY CABINET WAREROOMS
173 CHESTNUT STREET
PHILA:

2

1

2

3

UMBRELLA-MAKER.

UNDERTAKER.

UPHOLSTERER.

SHOEMAKER.

STATIONER.

TEA-DEALER.

LIQUOR-DEALER.

MACHINIST.

PAINTER.

PAPER-HANGER.

PAWNBROKER.

PERFUMER.

PHOTOGRAPHER.

PIANO-MAKER.

PLUMBER.

PRINTER.

RESTAURANT.

SASH-MAKER.

SCALE-MAKER.

SEWING MACHINE.

HOSIER.

JEWELLER.

LAMP-MAKER.

CABINET-MAKER.

DENTIST.

LIQUOR-DEALER.

CHAIR-MAKER.

COMB-DEALER.

MARBLE-WORKER.

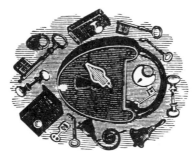

LOCKSMITH.

LUMBER-DEALER.

MACHINIST.

CHINA-WARE.

CLOCK AND WATCH-MAKER.

COAL-DEALER.

SHELL-FISH DEALER.

TINSMITH.

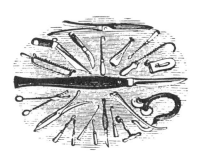

SURGICAL INSTRUMENTS.

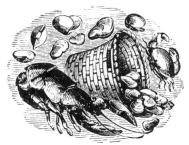

SHOEMAKER.

BAKER.

BLINDS AND SHADES.

CONFECTIONER.

COPPERSMITH.

CUTLER.

DRY GOODS.

FARRIER.

FISH-DEALER.

FLORIST.

FLOUR-DEALER.

FRAME-MAKER.

GAS-FITTER.

GENTLEMEN'S FURNISHER.

GROCER.

HAIR-DRESSER.

HARDWARE.

HARNESS-MAKER.

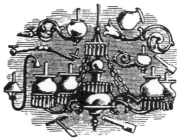

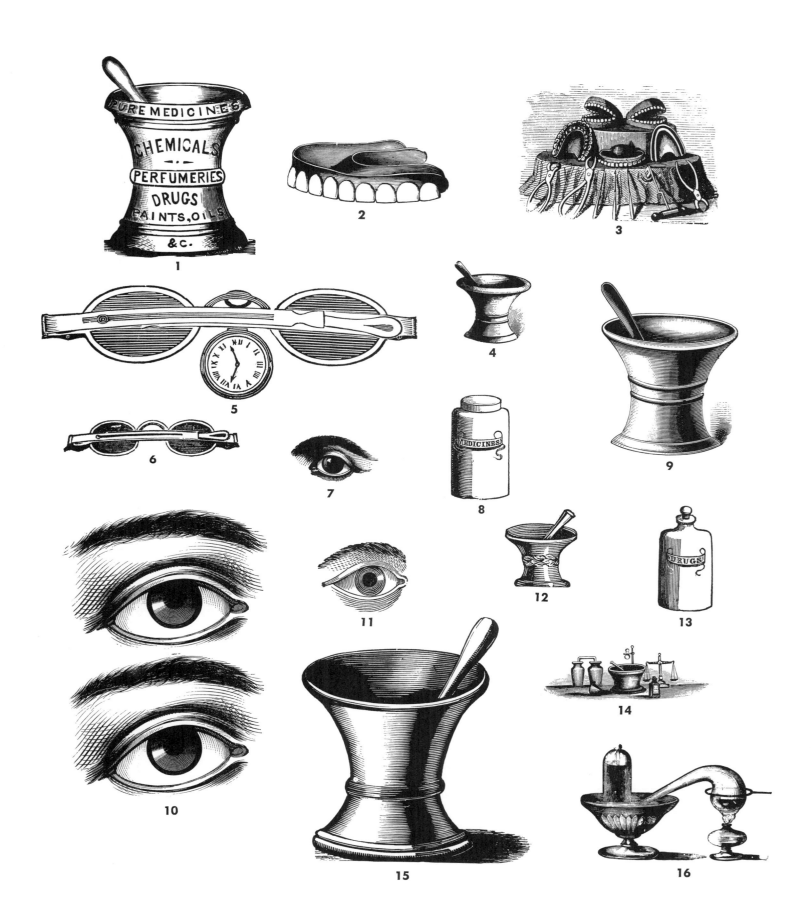

1

2

3

4

5

6

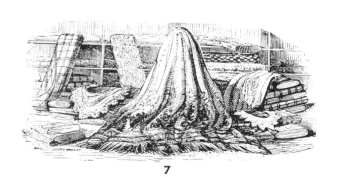

7

8

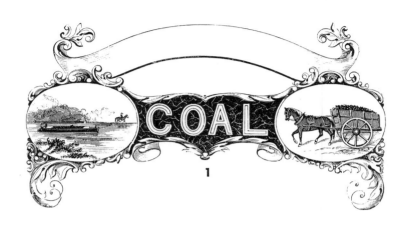

1

2

3

4

5

6

7

1

2

3

4

5

6

7

8

9

10

11

12

13

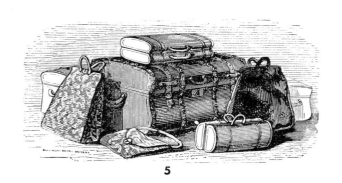

1

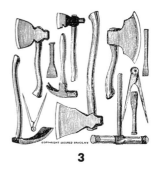

2

3

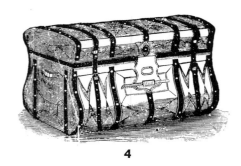

4

5

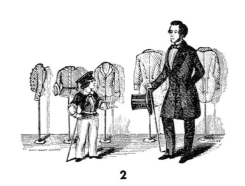

6

7

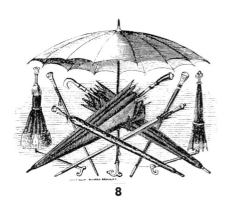

8

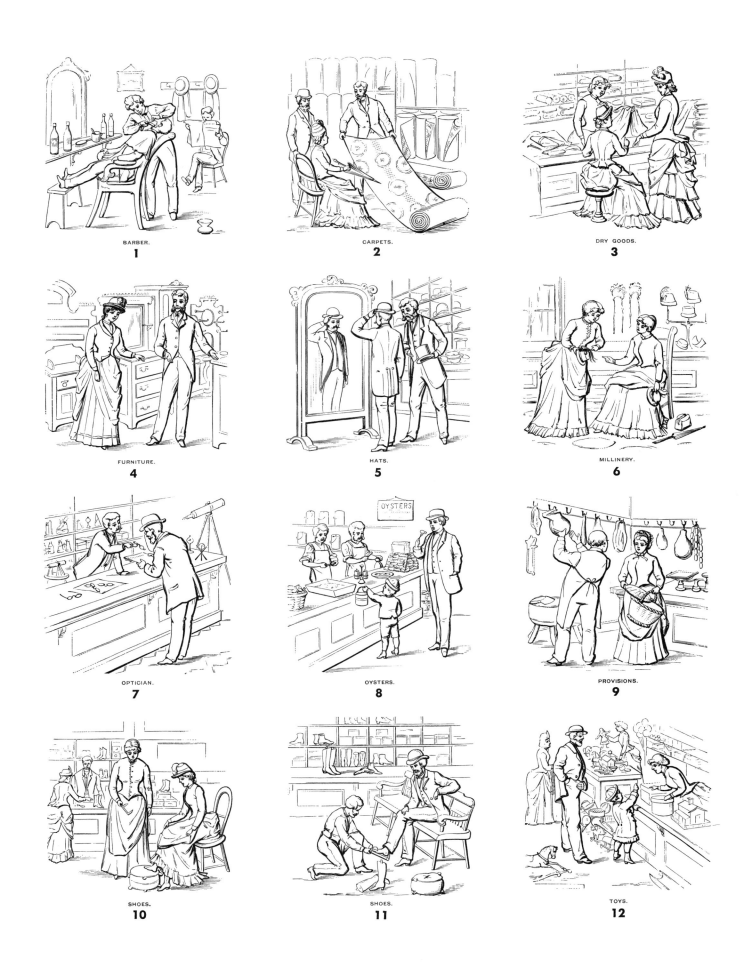

BARBER.
1

CARPETS.
2

DRY GOODS.
3

FURNITURE.
4

HATS.
5

MILLINERY.
6

OPTICIAN.
7

OYSTERS.
8

PROVISIONS.
9

SHOES.
10

SHOES.
11

TOYS.
12

1

2

HARDWARE

3

CUTLER

4

5

YOUNG HYSON

TEA

FINE BLACK TEAS

6

FRESH TEAS.

7

8

FRESH TEAS.

9

FRESH TEAS.

10

BLACK

GENUINE TEAS.

GREEN

1

2

3

4

5

6

7

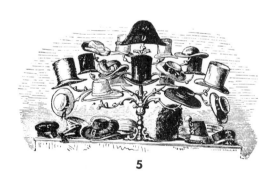

8

Manufacturer of and Dealer in

FLUID AND OIL CHANDELIERS,

DEALERS IN ALL KINDS OF

IRON AND STEEL,

WILLIAM WHITE,

PRINTER TO THE STATE,

COUNTING ROOM.   PRESS ROOM.

BOOK, NEWSPAPER, JOB, CARD AND ORNAMENTAL

PRINTER,

CORNER OF SPRING LANE & DEVONSHIRE STREET,

BOSTON, MASS.

JOB ROOM

COMPOSITION ROOM.

OAK HALL CLOTHING HOUSE,

PUBLISHERS, BOOKSELLERS AND STATIONERS,

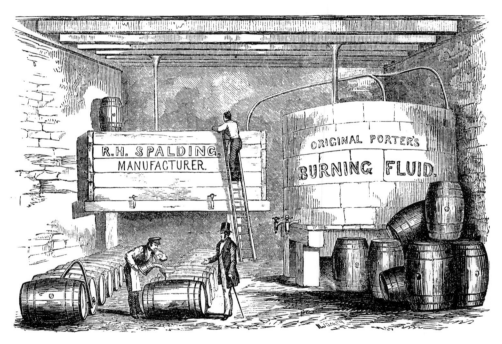

THOMPSON'S
[FORMERLY BLAKE'S,]
BONNET BLEACHERY
AND MANUFACTORY,
360½ WASHINGTON STREET, 360½
A few doors north of Essex St., over Tewksbury's Book Store.
BOSTON.

Every variety of Straw and Fancy Bonnets altered to fashionable shapes, cleansed and pressed in the very best manner.   Also, Gentlemen's Summer Hats.   Straw Bonnets Colored.   Milliners furnished with Bonnet Blocks of the latest patterns.
Goods forwarded by Express, &c., will receive immediate attention.

THE MOST COMPLETE ESTABLISHMENT IN THE UNITED STATES.

Alievi Enrico,

Riding Master.

THE BOSTON RIDING ACADEMY,

Era Works, Atlantic Docks, Brooklyn.

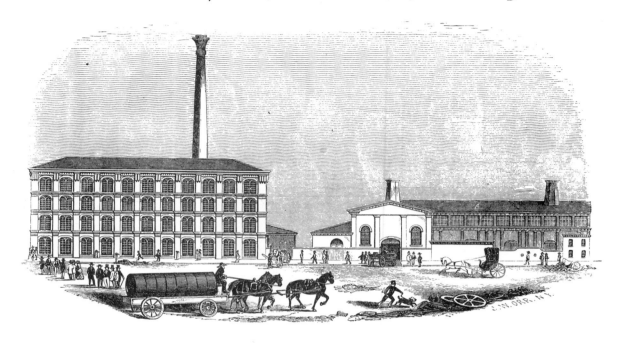

MANUFACTORY OF

GWYNNE'S PUMPING ENGINE,

SARGENT HARLOW, & Co.

SINGER'S SEWING MACHINES,

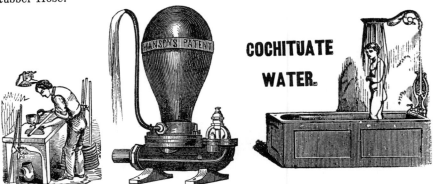

BROAD CLOTHS, CASSIMERES,

HARD AND SOFT COAL,

JOHN GOVE & COMPANY'S CLOTHING HOUSE,

UNITED STATES HOTEL, PHILADELPHIA,
C. J. MACLELLAN, PROPRIETOR.

BLAKE'S PATENT
FIRE-PROOF PAINT,

T. CUNNINGHAM, Manufacturer of Low & High Pressure Steam Boilers, of every description, Ships' Tanks, Coal Bunkers, Gasometers, &c. &c.

WATER STREET, Near Warren Bridge, Charlestown, Mass.

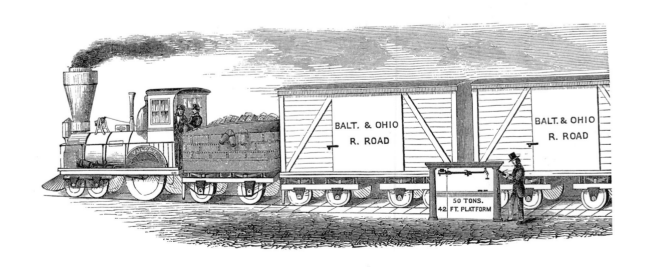

ALL KINDS OF
OMNIBUSES
MANUFACTURED BY
JOHN STEPHENSON
NEW-YORK.

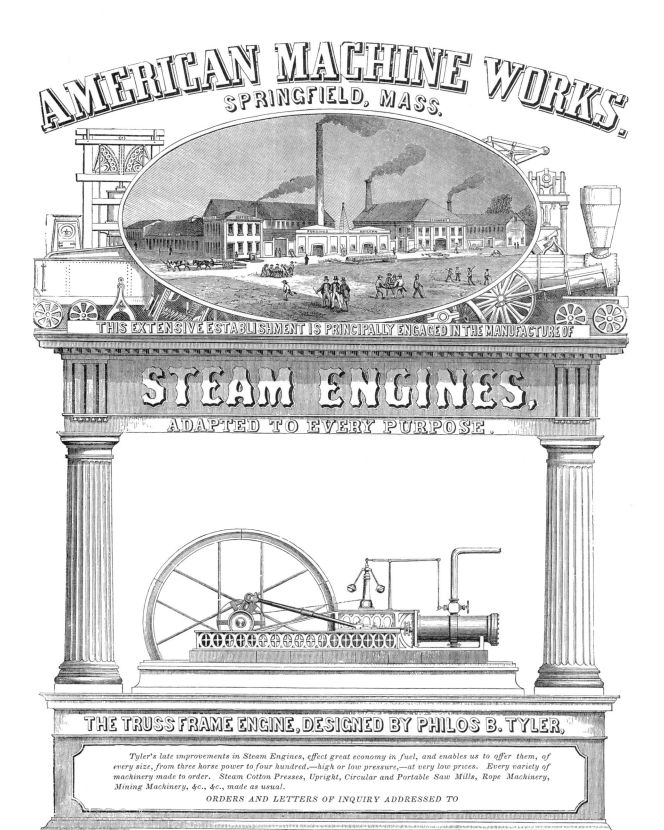

AMERICAN MACHINE WORKS.
SPRINGFIELD, MASS.

THIS EXTENSIVE ESTABLISHMENT IS PRINCIPALLY ENGAGED IN THE MANUFACTURE OF

STEAM ENGINES,
ADAPTED TO EVERY PURPOSE.

THE TRUSS FRAME ENGINE, DESIGNED BY PHILOS B. TYLER,

Tyler's late improvements in Steam Engines, effect great economy in fuel, and enables us to offer them, of every size, from three horse power to four hundred,—high or low pressure,—at very low prices. Every variety of machinery made to order. Steam Cotton Presses, Upright, Circular and Portable Saw Mills, Rope Machinery, Mining Machinery, &c., &c., made as usual.

ORDERS AND LETTERS OF INQUIRY ADDRESSED TO

PHILOS B. TYLER, PRES.T

37 E

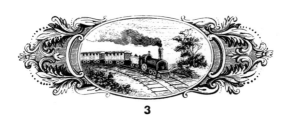

1

2

3

4

5

6

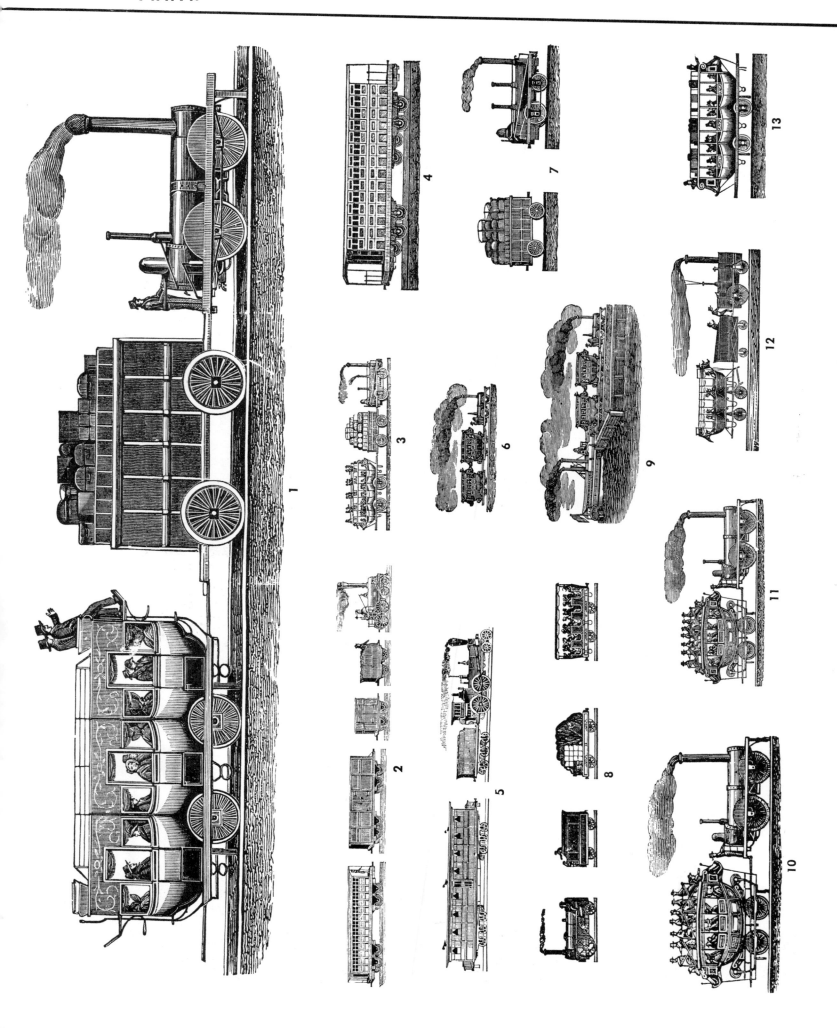

NOTES ON THE PLATES

Plate 12. ANIMALS. *Fig. 1*, Narwhal; *Fig. 2*, Zebra; *Fig. 3*, Vicuña; *Fig. 4*, Jaguar; *Fig. 5*, Polar Bear; *Fig. 6*, Hippopotamus; *Fig. 7*, Wolf; *Fig. 9*, Coati-mundi; *Fig. 10*, Whale; *Fig. 11*, Rabbits; *Fig. 12*, Rhinoceros; *Fig. 13*, Sheep; *Fig. 14*, Turtle; *Fig. 15*, Wildcat; *Fig. 16*, Tapir; *Fig. 17*, Tiger.

Plate 13. ANIMALS. *Fig. 1*, Dromedary; *Fig. 2*, Ant eater; *Fig. 3*, Beaver; *Fig. 4*, Cat; *Fig. 5*, Whalebone whale; *Fig. 6*, Reindeer; *Fig. 7*, Bear; *Fig. 8*, Leopard; *Fig. 9*, Kangaroo; *Fig. 10*, Lynx; *Fig. 11*, Fox; *Fig. 12*, Giraffe; *Fig. 13*, Ibex.

Plate 14. ANIMALS. *Fig. 1*, Bull; *Fig. 2*, Gazelle; *Fig. 3*, Bull; *Fig. 4*, Fox; *Fig. 5*, Goat; *Fig. 6*, Deer; *Fig. 7*, Kangaroo; *Fig. 8*, Bobcat; *Fig. 9*, Elephant; *Fig. 10*, Pig; *Fig. 11*, Horse; *Fig. 12*, Lion; *Fig. 13*, Antelope; *Fig. 14*, Gnu.

Plate 16. ANIMALS. *Fig. 1*, Cow; *Fig. 2*, Bear; *Fig. 4*, Bobcat; *Fig. 5*, Dromedary; *Fig. 6*, Sheep; *Fig. 7*, Donkey; *Fig. 8*, Bison; *Fig. 9*, Lion.

Plate 17. ANIMALS. *Fig. 1*, Racoon; *Fig. 2*, Deer and Dogs; *Figs. 3, 4*, Donkey; *Fig. 5*, Racoon; *Fig. 6*, Dog.

Plate 18. ANIMALS. *Fig. 2*, Tiger; *Fig. 3*, Elk; *Fig. 10*, Bear; *Fig. 11*, Lion; *Fig. 12*, Rat; *Fig. 13*, Bison.

Plate 19. ANIMALS. *Fig. 1*, Bison; *Fig. 2*, Donkey; *Fig. 3*, Cow; *Fig. 4*, Goat; *Fig. 5*, Elk; *Fig. 6*, Leopard; *Fig. 7*, Ibex; *Fig. 8*, Goat; *Fig. 9*, Zebra; *Fig. 10*, Antelope; *Fig. 11*, Moose; *Fig. 12*, Camel; *Fig. 13*, Walrus; *Fig. 14*, Monkey; *Figs. 15, 16*, Elephant; *Fig. 17*, Racoon.

Plate 23. AUTOMOBILES. *Fig. 1*, H. Mueller Mfg. 1896; *Fig. 2*, Locomobile 1918; *Fig. 3*, Pope-Toledo 1907.

Plate 24. AUTOMOBILES. *Fig. 1*, Packard 1908; *Fig. 2*, Molini 1911; *Fig. 3*, Packard 1913.

Plate 25. AUTOMOBILES. *Fig. 1*, Pope-Waverly 1907; *Fig. 3*, Overland 1908 H.A.

Plate 26. AUTOMOBILES. *Fig. 1*, Detroit 1907; *Figs. 3-5*, Haynes, 1923; *Fig. 6*, White 1913; *Fig. 7*, Reo 1913.

Plate 27. AUTOMOBILES. *Fig. 1*, Overland 1915; *Fig. 2*, Stanhope 1915; *Fig. 3*, Bell 1921; *Fig. 4*, Packard 1908.

Plate 28. AUTOMOBILES. *Fig. 1*, Chalmers 1909; *Fig. 2*, Studebaker Electric 1903; *Fig. 3*, ca 1895; *Fig. 4*, Ford 1907.

Plate 29. AUTOMOBILES. *Fig. 1*, Ford 1915; *Fig. 2*, Dayton; *Fig. 4*, Franklin 1918.

Plate 30. AUTOMOBILES. *Fig. 1*, Winton 1915; *Fig. 2*, International Harvester 1915; *Fig. 3*, Friedman Road Wagon 1901-2; *Fig. 4*, Herresford 1911.

Plate 31. BIRDS AND FOWL. *Fig. 1*, Bird of Paradise; *Fig. 2*, Flamingo; *Fig. 5*, Barn Owl; *Figs. 6, 7*, Owls; *Fig. 8*, Woodcock; *Fig. 9*, Hawk; *Fig. 10*, Swan; *Fig. 12*, Ostrich; *Fig. 13*, Flamingo.

Plate 33. BIRDS AND FOWL. *Fig. 4*, Peacock; *Fig. 6*, Quail; *Fig. 7*, Auk; *Fig. 8*, Toucan; *Fig. 9*, Robin; *Fig. 10*, Parrot; *Fig. 11*, Avocet.

Plate 34. BIRDS AND FOWL. *Fig. 1*, Wild Turkey; *Fig. 5*, Quail; *Fig. 6*, Hawk; *Fig. 7*, Woodpecker; *Fig. 8*, Canary; *Fig. 9*, Swan; *Fig. 10*, Baltimore Oriole.

Plate 35. BIRDS AND FOWL. *Fig. 1*, Dove; *Fig. 2*, Wren; *Fig. 3*, Pheasant; *Fig. 4*, Heron; *Figs. 6, 10*, Owl; *Fig. 8*, Pigeon.

Plate 46. CHRISTMAS. *Fig. 1* by Thomas Nast.

Plate 47. CHRISTMAS. *Figs. 1, 3* by Tomas Nast.

Plate 48. CHRISTMAS. *Figs. 1, 5* by Thomas Nast.

Plate 50. CHRISTMAS. *Fig. 3* by Thomas Nast.

Plate 52. CHRISTMAS. *Figs. 1-4, 6-8* reproduced through the courtesy of the New York Historical Society (Landauer Collection); *Fig. 5* by Thomas Nast.

Plate 53. CHRISTMAS. *Figs. 1-3, 5-8* reproduced through the courtesy of the New York Historical Society (Landauer Collection); *Fig. 4* by Thomas Nast.

Plate 54. CHRISTMAS. *Fig. 1* by Thomas Nast; *Figs. 2, 4, 7* reproduced through the courtesy of the New York Historical Society (Landauer Collection).

Notes for Plates 103 through 115 prepared by Paul H. Downing.

Plate 103. HORSE DRAWN VEHICLES. *Fig. 1*, Horse-Car or Street-Car, the type used in New York City from 1845 until early 20th century; *Fig. 2*, "Double-decker" horse drawn R.R. car, mid 19th century; *Fig. 3*, Covered Wagon, early 19th century.

Plate 104. HORSE DRAWN VEHICLES. *Fig. 1*, Family Sleigh and Pair, 2nd half 19th century; *Fig. 2*, Albany Cutters and Family sleigh, 2nd half 19th century; *Fig. 3*, Ice Wagon, 1860-1910; *Fig. 4*, Coal Cart Dumping, 2nd half 19th century; *Fig. 5*, Barouche or Calash and Pair, about 1850; *Fig. 6*, Extension Top Phaeton, about 1860; *Fig. 7*, Coach and Pair, early 19th century, coachman on box, footman standing on hind platform; *Fig. 8*, Wagon, 19th century; *Fig. 9*, Stage Coach, early 19th century; *Fig. 10*, Runabout, 2nd half 19th century; *Fig. 11*, Coal-box Buggy (from the shape of the back of the body), 2nd half 19th century; *Fig. 12*, Trotting race with high wheel Sulkies, 2nd and 3rd quarters 19th century; *Fig. 13*, Albany Cutter, 2nd half 19th century; *Fig. 14*, Ice Wagon, 1860-1910; *Fig. 15*, Calash Coach and Barouche or Calash, 2nd half 19th century; *Fig. 16*, Coal Cart in motion; *Fig. 17*, Landau for State Occasions, 1st half 19th century.

Plate 105. HORSE DRAWN VEHICLES. *Fig. 1*, Park Drag, Four-in-hand coach, sometimes called a "Tally-ho";

Fig. 2, Farm or Work Wagon with removable body; *Fig. 3*, Conestoga Wagon, originated in the Conestoga Valley of Pennsylvania during the 2nd half of 18th century, continued in use over a hundred years; *Fig. 4*, Hearse, mid 19th century; *Fig. 5*, Omnibus, 1850 to 1910; *Fig. 6*, Stage Coach, early 19th century.

Plate 106. HORSE DRAWN VEHICLES. *Fig. 1*, Victoria (panel-boot type), a popular lady's carriage from 1775-1910; *Figs. 2, 3*, Landaulet, closed and open, the "convertible" of 1760-1910.

Plate 107. HORSE DRAWN VEHICLES. *Fig. 1*, Berlin Coach and Pair, coachman and groom on the box; *Fig. 2*, Park Drag, the Four-in-hand coach of Society from 1775 to 1920. It was popular for driving to the races or other out of door sporting events, and was erroneously called a "Tally-ho" by the *hoi polloi*.

Plate 108. HORSE DRAWN VEHICLES. *Fig. 1*, Vis-à-vis, late 19th-early 20th century; *Fig. 2*, Physician's Phaeton, 1875-1910.

Plate 109. HORSE DRAWN VEHICLES. *Fig. 1*, Victoria Sleigh, late 19th century-early 20th century; *Fig. 2*, Express Wagon, 1850-1910; *Fig. 3*, Stage Coach, mid 19th century; *Fig. 4*, Tandem driving. Not as easy at it looks. Indulged in by sporting men throughout the 19th century.

Plate 110. HORSE DRAWN VEHICLES. *Fig. 1*, Barouche, presented to General Lafayette by the Congress in 1824; *Fig. 2*, Skeleton Wagon, 2nd half 19th century used in trotting races; *Fig. 3*, Spider Phaeton, 1870-1910, an American carriage which found favor with our English cousins; *Fig. 4*, Concord Wagon, 2nd half 19th century.

Plate 111. HORSE DRAWN VEHICLES. *Fig. 1*, Rockaway, 1860-1880; *Fig. 2*, Milk Delivery Wagon, 1875-1910.

Plate 112. HORSE DRAWN VEHICLES. *Fig. 1*, Chaise, 1800-1880. This is the type of Oliver Wendell Holmes' "One-hoss Shay"; *Fig. 2*, Cut-under Basket Phaeton, 1880-1910, popular for lady's driving, the rumble or "dickey" seat was for the groom; *Fig. 3*, Buggy called "Jenny Lind" in honor of the great singer's visit to this country in 1855.

Plate 113. HORSE DRAWN VEHICLES. *Fig. 1*, Hearse, middle to late 19th century; *Fig. 2*, Stage Coach, early 19th century; *Figs. 3, 4*, Horse-Car or Street-Car, the type used in New York City from 1845 until early 20th century; *Fig. 5*, Improved Business Wagon, 1850-1900; *Fig. 6*, Mule-drawn Cotton Wagon, 19th century; *Fig. 7*, Surrey; *Fig. 8*, Stage Coach, nicknamed "The Football Coach" from the shape of the body, early 19th century.

Plate 114. HORSE DRAWN VEHICLES. *Fig. 1*, Cart with mule or ass, 19th century; *Fig. 2*, Wagon, 1850-1910; *Fig. 3*, Horse-Car or Street-Car, 1832-1850; *Figs. 4, 5*,

Horse and Cart, 19th century; *Fig. 6*, Coach and Chaise, early 19th century; *Fig. 7*, Runabout and Horse, 1860-1890; *Fig. 8*, Conestoga Wagon; *Fig. 9*, Coal Wagon raised by a hand crank to "shoot" its load, 2nd half 19th century and early 20th century; *Figs. 10, 11*, Coach, early 19th century; *Fig. 12*, Omnibus operating on Broadway, New York, 2nd quarter 19th century; *Fig. 13*, Gig, 19th century; *Fig. 14*, Coach, early 19th century; *Fig. 15*, Butcher's Cart, 1850-1910.

Plate 115. HORSE DRAWN VEHICLES. *Fig. 1*, Jump-seat Barouche, 1860-1880. Carriage arranged with single seat for two passengers; *Fig. 2*, The same carriage with seats rearranged so that it may accommodate four passengers.

Plate 150. PORTRAITS. *Fig. 1*, Andrew Jackson.

Plate 152. PORTRAITS. *Fig. 1*, U. S. Grant; *Fig. 4*, Columbus; *Fig. 5*, Shakespeare; *Fig. 6*, William T. Sherman.

Plate 153. REPTILES, FISH, INSECTS. *Fig. 1*, Queen honeybee; *Fig. 2*, Drone honeybee; *Fig. 3*, Worker honeybee; *Fig. 4*, Crab; *Fig. 5*, Flea; *Fig. 6*, Marine turtle; *Figs. 7, 8*, Moth; *Fig. 9*, Beetle; *Fig. 10*, Butterfly; *Fig. 11*, Dragonfly; *Fig. 12*, Tussah moth; *Fig. 13*, Housefly; *Fig. 14*, Bluecrab; *Fig. 15*, Diamond back terrapin; *Fig. 16*, Lizzard; *Fig. 17*, Alligator; *Fig. 18*, Rattlesnake; *Fig. 19*, Sea robin; *Fig. 20*, Cowrie shell.

Plate 154. REPTILES, FISH, INSECTS. *Fig. 1*, Shrimp; *Fig. 2*, Crayfish; *Fig. 3*, Pike; *Fig. 4*, Weakfish; *Fig. 5*, Herring; *Fig. 6*, Oyster; *Fig. 9*, Porgy; *Fig. 10*, Frog; *Fig. 11*, Cod; *Fig. 12*, Sea turtle; *Fig. 13*, Box turtle; *Fig. 14*, Lobster; *Fig. 15*, Crocodile; *Fig. 16*, Crab; *Fig. 17*, Scorpion.

Plate 178. SYMBOLS AND EMBLEMS. *Fig. 1*, Knights of Golden Eagle; *Fig. 2*, United States; *Fig. 6*, New Jersey; *Fig. 7*, Pennsylvania; *Fig. 9*, Sons of St. George; *Fig. 10*, New York.

Plate 179. SYMBOLS AND EMBLEMS. *Fig. 1*, Argentina; *Fig. 2*, South Carolina; *Fig. 3*, New York; *Fig. 4*, Masonic; *Fig. 5*, Missouri.

Plate 180. SYMBOLS AND EMBLEMS. *Fig. 1*, Florida; *Fig. 2*, Foresters; *Fig. 3*, Nevada; *Fig. 4*, Peru; *Fig. 5*, Argentina; *Fig. 7*, Massachusetts; *Fig. 9*, Order of Red Men.

Plate 181. SYMBOLS AND EMBLEMS. *Fig. 2*, Portugal; *Fig. 3*, Peru.

Plate 182. SYMBOLS AND EMBLEMS. *Figs. 6, 9-15*, Masonic; *Fig. 8*, Elks.

Plate 183. SYMBOLS AND EMBLEMS. *Figs. 1-3*, Odd Fellows; *Fig. 4*, Mexico; *Fig. 6*, Temple of Honor; *Fig. 7*, Grand Army of the Republic; *Fig. 8*, Foresters.

The major sources of illustrations are type specimen books prior to 1890. Because the illustrations appear frequently in different catalogues and different years, the publisher believes that no useful or scholarly purpose is served by giving the exact source since no effort was made to reproduce or investigate their first appearance.

The following specimen catalogues were the main sources for this collection:

MacKellar, Smiths and Jordan.

White, John T. NEW YORK TYPE FOUNDRY SPECIMEN OF PRINTING TYPES CAST.

A. Zeese and Company.

James Conner's Sons.

Blomgren and Co.

Phelps Dalton and Co.

The following sources were also used:

Scrapbooks of the works of Dr. Alexander Anderson in the New York Public Library.

BALLOU'S PICTORIAL DRAWING-ROOM COMPANION.

HORSELESS AGE.

The Landauer Collection in the New York Historical Society.

THOMAS NAST'S CHRISTMAS DRAWINGS OF THE HUMAN RACE. Harper and Bros. 1890.

The material in the section of the Typographical and Ornamental Volume devoted to Alphabets and Decorative Initials was taken from the following books:

DECORATIVE INITIAL LETTERS, collected and arranged by A. F. Johnson:

Plates 165, 166, 168 to 170, 172 to 192, 214 to 216 (all inclusive)

SCHRIFTEN ATLAS, a collection made by Ludwig Petzendorfer, 1889:

Plates 194 to 197, 200 to 202, 206 to 210 (all inclusive)

EARLY WOODCUT INITIALS, selected and annotated by Oscar Jennings, M.D., in 1908:

Plates 167 and 171

SPECIMENS OF ELECTROTYPES, A. Zeese & Co., 1891:

Plates 193, 211 to 213 (inclusive)

PRANG'S STANDARD ALPHABETS, L. Prang & Co., 1878:

Plate 203

COPLEY'S PLAIN AND ORNAMENTAL STANDARD ALPHABETS, drawn and arranged by Frederick S. Copley, 1870:

Plates 198 and 199

OEUVRES DE JEAN MIDOLLE, published by Emile Simon Fils, Strasbourg, 1834-1835:

Plates 204 and 205

The plates of Trade Advertisements in the Pictorial Volume were taken from

AMERICAN PORTRAIT GALLERY, 1855

ILLUSTRATED AMERICAN ADVERTISER, 1856

The following check-list from the catalogue files of the Typographic Library of Columbia University, New York, represents the most complete collection of specimen books in America. The volumes were gathered by the late Henry Lewis Bullen, acting as curator and collector for the American Type Founders Company.

ALBANY TYPE FOUNDRY, R. Starr & Co., 1826.

BALTIMORE TYPE FOUNDRY, (Fielding Lucas, Jr., agent) 1832.

" " " F. Lucas, 1851.
" " " Lucas Brothers, 1854.
" " " H. L. Pelouze & Son, 1879.

BINNEY & RONALDSON, Philadelphia, 1809.
" " " 1812.

JAMES RONALDSON, Philadelphia, 1816
" " " 1822.

BOSTON TYPE FOUNDRY, 1820.
" " " 1825.
" " " 1826, (John Rogers, agent)
" " " 1828.
" " " 1832.
" " " 1837.
" " " 1845.
" " " John K. Rogers & Co., 1853.
" " " " " " 1856.
" " " " " " 1857.
" " " " " " 1860.
" " " " " " 1864.
" " " " " " 1867.
" " " " " " 1869.
" " " " " " 1871.

BOSTON TYPE FOUNDRY, John K. Rogers & Co., 1874.
" " " " " " c. 1875.
" " " " " " 1878.
" " " " " " 1880.
" " " " " " 1883.

BRUCE, DAVID & GEORGE, New York, 1815.
" " " " " 1815-16.
" " " " " 1818.

CHANDLER, A., New York, 1822.

CINCINNATI TYPE FOUNDRY, O. & H. Wells, 1827.
" " " " " 1834.
" " " (Horace Wells, agent) 1844.
" " " (L. T. Wells, agent) 1851.
" " " " " 1852.
" " " " " c. 1853.
" " " " " 1856.

CONNER & COOKE, New York, 1834.
" " " " 1836.
" " " " 1837.
" " (Supplement to the 1836 book)

JAMES CONNER & SON, New York, 1841.
" " " " " 1850.
" " " " " 1852.
" " " " " before 1855.
" " " " " 1855.
" " " " " 1859.
" " " " " 1860.

JAMES CONNER'S SONS, New York, 1870.
" " " " " 1876.
" " " " " 1885.
" " " " " 1888.
" " " " " 1891.

DICKENSON TYPE FOUNDRY, (Samuel N. Dickenson) Boston, 1842.
" " " (Samuel N. Dickenson) Boston, 1847.
" " " (Phelps and Dalton) Boston, 1855.

FRANKLIN TYPE FOUNDRY, Allison, Smith & Johnson, Cincinnati, 1871.
" " " " 1873.

FRANKLIN LETTER-FOUNDRY, A. W. Kinsley & Company, Albany, 1829.

HAGAR, WILLIAM & CO., New York, 1826.
" " " " " 1831.
" " " " " 1841.
" " " " " 1850
" " " " " 1854.
" " " " " 1858.
" " " " " 1860.
" " " " " 1873.
" " " " " 1886.

JOHNSON & SMITH, Phila., 1834.
(Successors to Binney and Ronaldson
" " " 1841.
" " " 1843.

LAWRENCE JOHNSON, Philadelphia, 1844
" " " c. 1845.

LAWRENCE JOHNSON & CO., Phila., 1847.
" " " " 1849.
" " " " before 1853.
" " " " 1853.
" " " " 1856.
" " " " 1857.
" " " " 1859.
" " " " 1865.

MAC KELLAR, SMITHS & JORDAN, Phila., 1868.
" " " " 1869.
" " " " 1871.
" " " " 1873.
" " " " 1876.
" " " " 1877.
" " " " 1878.
" " " " 1881.
" " " " 1882.
" " " " 1884.
" " " " 1885.
" " " " 1886.
" " " " 1887.
" " " " 1888.
" " " " 1889.
" " " " 1890.
" " " " 1892.
" " " " 1894.

MAC KELLAR, SMITHS & JORDAN, Phila., 1895.
" " " " 1897.

LOTHIAN, GEORGE B., New York, 1841.

LYMAN, NATHAN & COMPANY, Buffalo, 1841.
" " " " 1853.

NEW ENGLAND TYPE FOUNDRY, Henry Willis, Boston, 1834.
" " " " George and J. Curtis, Boston, 1838.
" " " " " 1841.

OHIO TYPE FOUNDRY, Guilford & Jones, Cincinnati, 1851.

PELOUZE, LEWIS, Philadelphia, 1849.

PELOUZE, LEWIS & SON, Philadelphia, 1856.

REICH, STARR & COMPANY, Philadelphia, 1818.

ROBB & ECKLIN, Philadelphia, 1836.

ALEXANDER ROBB, Philadelphia, 1844.

STARR & LITTLE, Albany, 1828.

WHITE, ELIHU, New York, 1812.
" " " " 1817.
" " " " 1821.
" " " " 1826.
" " " " 1829.

Numbers in boldface refer to pages and numbers following slash refer to specific figures on the page. Roman numerals refer to introductory text.